CONTACT FRONT

*Proven Leadership Lessons from
the Iraq War's Deadliest Battle*

Barry Shaw

NEWMAN SPRINGS PUBLISHING
320 Broad Street
Red Bank, NJ 07701

First originally published by Newman Springs Publishing 2024

ISBN 979-8-88763-867-6 (Paperback)
ISBN 979-8-88763-868-3 (Digital)

Printed in the United States of America

To the marines who came before me, who set the bar so high,
my futile attempts to reach it somehow proved adequate.

Contents

Introduction

The United States Marine Corps is one of the finest fighting forces the world has ever known. In a day and age that sometimes conflicts with traditions and legacies of the past, the marine corps relentlessly pursues the high standards written in blood and established through the sacrifices of marines in battles from long ago. Nothing articulates these ethos better than a quote from Marine Lt. Col. John Thomason, who said,

> There is nothing particularly glorious about sweaty fellows, laden with killing tools, going along to fight. All that is behind those men is in that column too: the old battles, long forgotten, that secured our nation; traditions of things endured and things accomplished, such as regiments hand down forever.

The legacy and fighting traditions of the marine corps are as strong today as they have ever been. Propelled by the momentum of tough, deadly, hard-fought battles long forgotten by the nation, today's marines continue the prestigious mission to win America's battles.

Winning battles is the marine corps' highest priority. Every aspect of the marine corps serves the sole purpose to provide support and solutions to the individual marine charged with engaging the enemy in deadly combat. The aspect that contributes to the marine corps' success in battle is effective leadership. The marine corps' long-standing tradition of success relies heavily on sound leadership principles and methodologies that have been tested and proven under the harshest conditions imaginable. Success in such conditions rests solely on the availability of effective leadership. There is not a more fitting proving ground for leadership methods than the battlefield where the relentless grind of war transpires.

This book will explain leadership concepts for success in any environment. The same concepts, methods, and implementations that result in victory during battle also result in victory inside a boardroom, during a sales presentation, or while coordinating a company merger. These leadership concepts that were proven and relied upon during the Iraq War's deadliest battle, the Second Battle of Fallujah, are based on personal experiences that took place in and around Fallujah in November 2004.

I am writing this book more than fifteen years after the battle because it has taken this long to process the experience. This book could never have been written until now. It has taken years to decipher, evaluate, comprehend, and conceptualize my experiences in Iraq. Context and hindsight, along with years of personal and professional growth, have provided the confidence to articulate successful leadership concepts anyone can use to achieve success. I continue to use and teach these same concepts today as a supervisor for a large state law enforcement agency.

The leadership concepts included here are those I have come to value after years of reflection coupled with careful consideration of what is relevant to success in any chosen profession. My own accomplishments are by no means extraordinary, nor have I invented some new approach to leadership. The concepts presented are my interpretation of what worked, what currently works, and what is necessary for developing future effective leaders. Each leadership concept is easily implemented at any level and applies to every discipline. The perspective of a young marine sergeant thrust into an unexpected leadership role on the eve of the bloodiest battle of the war in Iraq will be coupled with context gained from years of reflection, evaluation, and professional development.

The courage, valor, and sacrifice displayed by the marines and soldiers who fought in the vicious streets of Fallujah were and still are astonishing to me. My combat experience does not compare to the extraordinary acts of heroism on constant display in and around Fallujah and the entire Anbar Province during the fall of 2004, but they do hopefully provide some context and relevancy for the selected leadership concepts. God bless the brave souls of those marines and soldiers who gave the ultimate sacrifice in service of their nation, and God bless the Gold Star Families they left behind.

Chapter 1

Bad Karmah

November 15, 2004. A loud explosion broke the silence and shook the earth under our feet. Instantly, a huge cloud of dust and smoke began to climb high and dim the clear blue sky. The blast was only two hundred meters south of our position on the main supply route leading into Al-Karmah, Iraq. Way too close for comfort, marines began scrambling to their armored vehicles for the inevitable response to provide security for the ground medical evacuation of the wounded. Security was a high priority because insurgents would often attempt to exploit an improvised explosive attack by ambushing the US forces responding to the scene.

At this time in Iraq, all medevacs had to be completed on the ground, traveling the same dangerous roads where the initial casualties had occurred. US aircraft were restricted from flying during daylight hours because the threat from small arms fire and rocket-propelled grenade attacks was too great.

A section of LAV-25s would respond to assess the damage from the blast and provide security for the medevac. LAV-25s are light armored vehicles equipped with a twenty five millimeter main gun, additionally equipped with two 7.62-millimeter machine guns, a crew of three marines responsible for operating the vehicle, and four specially trained infantry scouts to provide security and conduct dismounted operations. I was a vehicle commander for a LAV-25, responsible for the vehicle, crew, and scouts.

By the fall of 2004, our unit was made up of experienced veterans of the intense urban combat that had been taking place in and around Fallujah. We instantly recognized the blast as an improvised explosive device. IEDs were the biggest threat to the marine and army units working to restore stability in the war-torn area of Iraq known as the Sunni Triangle. IEDs were typically constructed from artillery or mortar shells and either command detonated through a hardwired trigger held by the enemy or remote detonated by an insurgent using a cellular phone or other electronic device hiding in the distance, waiting to ambush US Forces.

Some IEDs were crudely constructed from hollow metal objects like pieces of pipe or vehicle driveshafts and stuffed with a plastic explosive charge, nails, nuts, bolts, etc. Though sometimes crudely constructed, IEDS were always dangerous and capable of sending superheated razor-sharp metal flying through the air fast enough to penetrate armored vehicles. IEDs could easily burn, maim a person, and kill anyone within the effective blast radius no matter the precautions.

At the time of the blast, the Light Armored Reconnaissance Platoon I was assigned to was tasked with guarding two strategic bridges on one of only two main supply routes that accessed the city of Fallujah from the north. Sandwiched between two small towns, Qaryat ash Shahabi and Al-Karmah, were two small bridges over irrigation ditches that carried significant strategic importance. The bridges were necessary to keep the US supply route intact so personnel and equipment could move freely. If left unprotected, insurgents could easily destroy the bridges and further restrict US movement in and around Fallujah. The bridges were about 150 meters apart with the city of Al-Karmah to the north and Qaryat ash Shahabi to the south. The mission, terrain, and enemy presence created a pressure cooker.

My section of two LAV-25s were first to leave the relative safety of our assembly area to assess the situation and provide aid. As we approached the blast site, we saw a US Army truck with a flatbed trailer that had been hauling a bulldozer. The truck was mangled and smoldering in the street. The streets were quiet and desolate, and nearby buildings seemed empty. An eerie feeling began to creep in as we approached the scene, the feeling that only combat soldiers know when things are about to go bad.

The toll of the heavy fighting that had taken place in the past was evident on the structures lining the road. Every building within two blocks of the main road showed the scars of combat: broken windows with jagged glass, doors with shattered locks swinging from hinges, and masonry walls riddled with bullet holes. The roads were scarred with deep craters from IEDs, artillery, and mortar shells. This area that had once been a well-populated, bustling area of commerce and life was now a war-torn battle space.

We shielded the destroyed army vehicle with our section of LAV-25s, and the platoon corpsman, Doc Cannon, began rendering medical attention to the two wounded soldiers who had been in the army truck. The soldiers had serious injuries to their faces and eyes from the windshield that was blown inward from the IED blast. As soon as our vehicles were in position, our scouts sprung from the safety of the LAV-25s to get to covered positions and provide security for the medevac operation and the rest of the unit. Armored vehicles in the urban environment have tremendous capabilities but are also susceptible to attacks from determined insurgents willing to close distance and engage in close-quarter battle. Scouts provide vital security to keep insurgents at a distance so the LAV's powerful thermal sights and superior firepower can be brought to bear effectively.

As soon as the scouts hit the ground, accurate small arms fire began impacting all around us. Enemy rounds flew past our heads with the sound of red-hot steel plunged into cold water. These were not the usual potshots fired wildly by insurgents meant to harass us with little chance of inflicting casualties. Our unit had become accustomed to that tactic and rarely blinked an eye. This was accurate automatic weapons fire, a bold attack initiated on by a large disabled vehicle that would take some time to secure and remove from the battle space.

Some of the scouts were able to leap and bound to adequate cover; others were pinned down, staying as low as possible with whatever cover or concealment they could muster. The bullets smashing into the LAV's hull sounded like someone pounding the side of the vehicle with a sledgehammer. I radioed to our company executive officer, "Black 5, this is Blue 2, *contact front.*"

Chapter 2

Contact Front

Knowing the scouts who hadn't made it to adequate cover were in serious danger, both LAV crews began frantically scanning the desolate urban landscape with thermal sights for heat signatures. The buildings and rubble to our front made it almost impossible to visually identify enemy positions. There were hundreds of places to hide. Enemy insurgents would engage from a concealed position and quickly move from one building to another using alternate entrances and exits to remain concealed, making it difficult to locate where enemy fire was originating. We knew the general vicinity, but pinpointing the exact position the fire was originating was virtually impossible.

Apprehensive for our exposed scouts, my LAV-25 began engaging enemy positions in the approximate vicinity of enemy fire. My gunner, Cpl. Adam McGing, whom we called Ginger, began pouring machine gun bursts into suspected enemy positions with the interior-mounted M240G machine gun. I stood up from the turret and did the same with the turret-mounted M240G machine gun.

As it always happens in these situations, time slows down, and training takes over. I instantly reverted back to my initial basic training on the M240G when I was an eighteen-year-old private. "The easiest way to shoot a proper twenty- to twenty-five-round burst is to get your sight picture," my sergeant instructor told us. "Squeeze the trigger and say to yourself, 'Die, motherf——r, die,' then let off the trigger." He was adamant that the desired twenty- to twenty-five-round burst would be achieved every time with this method. I engaged: sight picture, trigger press, "Die, motherf——r, die," let off, sight picture, trigger press, "Die, motherf——r, die," let off, sight picture, trigger press.

Our efforts worked, and enemy fire slowed and became less accurate. Our exposed scouts were able to move to covered positions and set up adequate security. One team of scouts soon radioed enemy fire was coming from a burned-out school bus that was partially blocking an intersection 150 meters to the south. Both LAVs launched a barrage of machine gun bursts into the bus. All enemy fire stopped.

With the enemy suppressed, the wounded soldiers were transported by Humvee to Camp Fallujah's trauma center, and the bulldozer was off-loaded and used to pull the demolished army truck back to our assembly area. During the same firefight, one of the scout teams identified an additional IED farther to the south near the intersection with the destroyed school bus. They were able to safely patrol to the device, establish security, and detonate the IED in place, no doubt saving American lives in the process.

During the two weeks our platoon secured the two strategic bridges, we would encounter eleven IEDs in and around Karmah. Some we found before the IEDs could be detonated. One was a dud that bellowed white smoke profusely when it was triggered by an insurgent as my vehicle drove past. Others rocked us to our core, wounding marines and soldiers and killing US Army sergeant Joe Nolan who was attached to us as an interpreter.

Contact front is one of the simplest examples of a contact report. Contact reports alert those who are being engaged or who are about to be engaged as to the general direction of where the immediate threat is located. Initial contact reports are typically hasty and communicated by simply shouting, "Contact!" *Contact* is then quickly followed with a general direction: front, rear, left, right, etc. The direction given during a contact report is always based on the direction of travel of the unit engaged. Once the direction of the threat is established, a response is initiated, and all available resources are dedicated to eliminating the threat. Contact reports come in many forms, and as time allows, more detailed contact reports are communicated to higher levels to delineate the battlefield.

Combat is the ultimate proving ground for leadership theory and practical application. Contact front means facing extreme challenges head-on. In combat, contact front means you are traveling directly into the enemy's position, or the enemy is attacking into your position. This is one of the most intense situations encountered on the battlefield. Time is of the essence, and tough decisions have to be made quickly in order to save lives, destroy the enemy, and accomplish the mission.

A lifetime of leadership lessons can be learned and engrained in a relatively short period of time because of the intensity, sacrifice, and rigorous pace combat demands. While leadership in combat may differ by tempo and risk, the process for preparation and development of combat leaders should in no way differ for leaders in any other discipline. Whether combat, athletics, law enforcement, or business, leaders must produce and influence action that contributes to the success of the overall mission in accordance with organizational values.

Hans von Seeckt said, "Action has three stages: the decision born of thought, the order or preparation for execution, and the execution itself. All three stages are governed by the will." For a leader to be successful, all three stages of action must be developed. *Contact front* is the resource that can help anyone develop all three stages of action in order to successfully lead and inspire people and organizations to accomplish the mission.[1]

In every organization, leaders will be faced with challenges. For true leaders, procrastination is never appropriate, failure is not an option, and recklessness must be avoided. The leadership concepts highlighted here have been proven in battle, developed over time, and prioritized so that when applied, any leader can be confident when he or she is alerted, "Contact front!"

---

[1] Hans von Seeckt, *Thoughts of a Soldier*, trans. Gilbert Waterhouse (London: Ernest Benn, 1930), 123.

Post engagement outside Fallujah: Off-loading the bulldozer to tow the damaged truck and trailer into the assembly area.

View of detonating an IED in place after an intense firefight south of Karmah, Iraq.

Chapter 3

Courage

By the time Alpha Company arrived in Kuwait, I had already been there for a month. I left Camp Lejeune in August of 2004 as a member of the advance party, a small group of marines who deploy ahead of the main body responsible for securing the gear brought to Kuwait by ship. A Marine Light Armored Reconnaissance Company's primary tool is the LAV-25. Each platoon consists of four LAV-25s augmented by a Headquarters and Weapons Platoon made up of other types of armored vehicles. Alpha Company consisted of approximately twenty-five to thirty armored vehicles and 145 marines.

In Kuwait, we made several trips to the port where our vehicles had been off-loaded. We convoyed the vehicles back to our staging area at Camp Udairi, a large base surrounded by uninhabited desert. It was used as a staging area for US troops going north into Iraq. Between trips to the port, we prepped our vehicles ahead of the main body's arrival, ensuring all equipment was operational. The rest of Alpha soon arrived. We remained in Kuwait for another week, acclimating to the intense heat, zeroing weapons, reviewing rules of engagement, and conducting rehearsals.

The day of departure arrived, and we made final preparations to enter Iraq. We were issued ammo, more ammo than I had ever seen before in one place. We were given so much ammo, it was a challenge to fit it all in the vehicle. Every nook and cranny was stuffed with topped-off magazines, belts of linked ammunition, rockets, grenades—you name it, we had it. Our company commander, Capt. John Griffin, had a priest sprinkle holy water on each vehicle. Not being Catholic, this was a new phenomenon to me, but I was happy to accept any help we could get. Captain Griffin issued the order with our instructions for movement into Iraq, culminating in Fallujah.

At sunset, Alpha Company pulled out of Camp Udairi. Our long column of vehicles pointed north. We made one last stop near the border and received a final briefing with the latest intelligence on possible enemy threats to convoys entering theater. Around midnight, we entered Iraq. We were now on our own and operating freely in a combat zone. I was a vehicle commander of a LAV-25 and the lead vehicle for Third (Blue) Platoon. Blue Platoon was also the lead platoon for the convoy. We were instructed to push out approximately five kilometers ahead of the main body and act as a reconnaissance element.

The night was very dark, and the space between vehicles and operating completely blacked out made for a lonely feeling. There was nothing but the unknown in front of us, and my platoon commander's vehicle was only visible through magnified night vision to our rear. It was as if a clock started ticking as soon as we crossed into Iraq, an imaginary internal timer counting the seconds until we would meet the enemy. Would it take days, weeks, or would it be at the next overpass?

We pushed north all night. The deeper we got into Iraq, the more frequent far-off firefights with red and green tracers volleying back and forth became. The smell of Iraq, now forever burned into my brain, became pervasive. A mix of burning shit, trash, and rubber—the smell would persist for the next eight months in an almost constant haze that served as a reminder this was not home.

After twelve hours on the road, we reached a resupply site where we refueled the vehicles, ate, and tried to sleep. Later in the day, a platoon from Delta Company, whom we were replacing in Fallujah, arrived. They would serve as our guide to Camp Baharia, a small base a few kilometers west of the much larger (and much nicer) Camp Fallujah. The platoon from Delta Company was less than thrilled about their current assignment. They had been hit by a roadside bomb on their way to link up with us, and one of their scouts had been seriously wounded. As we passed by, one of the Delta marines shouted, "Too bad you couldn't find the place on your own," as he was cleaning blood from his vehicle.

As darkness fell, we left the resupply site, with the Delta platoon leading our column of vehicles. We continued north until the main supply route we were on turned to the west just south of Baghdad. We eventually exited onto Route Mobile. In the coming months, we would become very familiar with the dangers of this section of highway. Tonight, it was quiet, and we traveled the infamous twenty-four-kilometer stretch of highway from Abu Gharib prison to Fallujah and into Camp Baharia, a bare-bones forward-operating base that housed us and an infantry battalion. When we arrived, that battalion was Second Battalion, First Marines (2/1), later replaced by Third Battalion, Fifth Marines (3/5), who would later serve as part of the main effort during the siege of Fallujah and participate in some of the most vicious urban combat in history. It was an honor to share space with such brave marines who shouldered such a heavy task.

Inside the walls and relative safety of Camp Baharia, we were reunited with some familiar faces. We all knew each other. We belonged to the same battalion back at Camp Lejeune and worked and trained alongside each other on a daily basis. Delta Company had been in Fallujah for approximately seven months already. They had the look of seasoned combat soldiers. Their gear was worn and permanently sweat stained, their bodies lean, and their faces weathered and tired.

I could tell the marines of Delta Company that I had known back at Camp Lejeune were not the same people; Fallujah had changed them; the experience had hardened them. They had seen heavy combat and suffered significant casualties, including a catastrophic explosion when an LAV-25 triggered an antitank mine while on patrol. Marines constructed a memorial in the company area with the names of the Delta marines who had been killed in action. Nearby, inside a makeshift chapel, one of the walls was covered with eight-by-ten photos of marines from 2/1 who had made the ultimate sacrifice. The faces, names, dog tags, and personal mementos served as a harsh reminder of the dangers now awaiting us.

We settled down and attempted to sleep. Delta Company still occupied the large white tent that we would eventually inhabit. Alpha Company slept outside on the ground. Soon, sounds of a distant gunfight filled the night air, an Iraqi lullaby the marines of Delta Company had long grown accustomed too—we, not so much. This was no training exercise. The shooting was not coming from a neighboring practice range back at Camp Lejeune. The sounds were of marines outside the wire, engaging the enemy. Small arms fire turned into heavy machine guns and belt-fed forty-millimeter grenades as the quick reaction force arrived. Finally, a C-130 gunship came on station and pounded the area with its twenty-five-millimeter Gatling gun, appearing as a giant red laser originating from the dark sky. The shooting stopped, and an unnerving calm filled the air. Staring into an unfamiliar sky, reality set in. I was scared.

Fear is something all combat soldiers are forced to reckon with. Fear of death, fear of failure, and fear of the unknown all must be overcome physically, mentally, and emotionally. No one is exempt. Every marine or soldier who has ever met the enemy in battle has felt fear. Fear is likely what brings combat veterans together. Though many would never admit it, fear created the "I know how you feel, I've been there," bond, brotherhood, and understanding that exists between combat veterans. Only a select few know what combat is really like. Books and movies can never replicate the experience because they lack the powerful and primitive emotion that has driven human existence for eternity. Shared fear is why combat soldiers can instantly connect, trust, and communicate with one another.

Fear is prominent in combat because of the obvious dangers associated with it, but fear is not exclusive to the battlefield. Both natural and manageable, fear exists in all aspects of life, in every profession, and can be one of the most debilitating factors in a person's performance or quest for improvement. Fear keeps people in their comfort zone; comfort zones cap potential by not allowing growth and development. Many people try to mask fear with excuses initiated by internal conversations to rationalize their fear into a false logic eventually accepted as truth. "I don't have time," "I will embarrass myself," "I could get hurt," "I will fail," are the usual culprits, little lies that accumulate and escalate over time, warping reality and crushing any chance at progress and success.

Fear is a lie and can be overcome with truth. Understanding the layers of fear and peeling them away with honest and unbiased rationale reveal the truth and identify necessary steps for success, simplifying the process. Instead of standing at the bottom of a seemingly overwhelming mountain, the mountain becomes a series of small steps that lead to the top, the desired end state. The discipline and willingness to face fear just long enough to visualize the necessary steps to accomplish the mission and initiate the required action is known as courage. American historian George F. Kennan beautifully captured the essence of courage in his quote, "Heroism is endurance for one moment more."

Courage is the ability to perform in the face of fear. Like most other intangible qualities, courage is a skill that can be developed and improved upon over time. Fear can be a powerful motivating factor if properly understood and internalized. Understanding the different types of fear and how to conquer them is key to using fear to your advantage instead of allowing it to be a crippling factor both personally and organizationally. Courage coupled with skill manifests into confidence. Confidence evaluated and screened for recklessness is dominant. Whether a marine conducting a combat mission, a batter with two on and two out in the bottom of the ninth, or a business executive poised to conduct a crucial sales presentation, each will feel fear, each will mask it a different way, and each should use it to their advantage.

Fear is complex, but excluding phobias, significant traumas, and anxiety disorders, and for the purpose of this book, fear can be categorized as emotional and physical. Physical fear is the body's physiological response to a known threat. This response is almost universal: increased heart rate, auditory exclusion, reduced cognitive ability, loss of fine motor skills, amplified strength, reduced blood flow to the extremities, and tunnel vision are all symptoms of physical fear. The body's physiological response to fear can only be overcome by the development of an overtrained response through thousands of repetitions replicating the situation being encountered. Negating the physiological symptoms of fear is usually only accomplished by highly trained professionals or a person who is deeply committed to mastering their craft. Fortunately, most people are not forced into life-and-death situations on a regular basis, and so they very rarely, if ever, feel all-out physical fear.

Emotional fear is by far the most common fear felt by people today. Emotional fear is a result of how a situation is interpreted by an individual, so it will differ drastically from person to person. The marine or soldier prepping for enemy contact or the adrenaline junky who craves seemingly dangerous activities both feel fear the same as anyone else, but they have learned to understand why they feel fear, identify the things they can do to mitigate real danger, and make a calculated decision to face their fear based on an honest assessment of risk and capability.

Personal courage occurs during the assessment of a perceived fear, and the legitimacy of the assessed fear is dependent on honesty throughout the process. Courage without capability is dangerous. Courage is not fearlessness, recklessness, or being carefree. Courage is refusing to shut down when faced with adversity. It is the willingness to stay in the pocket, feel the heat for a moment, then engage your brain instead of instantly surrendering and diving down the convenient and delusional path of skewed logic that leads to self-doubt, excuses, and failure.

Courage is not easy, though some people may make it look easy. Courage takes awareness, recognition and practice. Reading this chapter provides the awareness; recognition and practice take time and commitment. Some have been lying to themselves for so long and often, their excuses are accepted as truth and easily overlooked. This is where honesty when assessing fear and capability is critical. The thoughts, *I can't* or *I give up*, need to be carefully and honestly analyzed. Extreme inward honesty when evaluating fear and excuses will likely expose an "I can't" or "I give up" as an actual "I don't want to," "That would make me uncomfortable," or "I am lazy." This is where growth occurs; this is where character is formed and courage is developed.

Viktor Frankl, a Holocaust survivor and author, touches on this process in his timeless book *A Man's Search for Meaning*. Frankl documents his experiences and process for coping with the worst conditions fathomable when forced into Nazi concentration camps. He captures the fear and capability assessment process in his famous quote, "Between stimulus and response there is a space. In that space is our power to choose our response. In our response lies our growth and our freedom." Frankl exemplified courage by recognizing and exercising his power to choose his response with virtually zero capability, all while facing one of the most powerful and extreme evils to ever exist.

Frankl survived three years inside various Nazi concentration camps. He did it courageously but also calculatedly. Frankl was experiencing real fear, where every decision or action could be met with instant death. If he did not assess his capability honestly, he would have been severely punished or killed. Courage without careful and brutally honest evaluation can be dangerous when real danger exists. In the process of honestly evaluating fear, if it is determined that there is no or limited capability to mitigate the danger to an acceptable level, continuing results in blind courage and provides a recipe for disaster. Whether a Nazi concentration camp, combat, or any other high-stakes environment, there is a fine line between boldness and recklessness. Boldness is another term for calculated courage; recklessness will get you or your people killed or maimed when real danger is present.

Whether deciding to continue an assault after suffering casualties or choosing to start a weight loss plan, the process of evaluating fear and capability is the same. Both scenarios have consequence, both have reward, and both require courage. Honestly evaluating fear and capability is what allows you to use fear to your advantage by identifying the areas that need improvement. Recognizing and acknowledging the fear that keeps you from striving to be better no matter the task at hand is the first step to turning weakness into strength.

- Tired of being bullied or intimidated? Train in martial arts. Replicate the same fight or flight response felt when being bullied and intimidated but in a controlled and safe environment. Develop an overtrained response, increase your capability, and mitigate fear.

- Fear of public speaking holding you back professionally? Practice. Develop a keynote speech you are passionate about, rehearse it in the mirror, video it, and critique yourself to gain confidence. Sign up for a public speaking class or join a public speaking club.

- Overweight and out of shape but do not know how to start? Analyze your fear and determine the real reason you are scared to commit to a healthy lifestyle. Then visualize the small steps necessary to mitigate the fear, formulate a plan, and execute.

Emotional fear makes our personal weaknesses obvious to us and provides the path to self-improvement. Eliminating weakness mitigates fear by expanding capability and allowing an increased opportunity for success whenever faced with adversity.

Personal courage is necessary for anyone to effectively lead subordinates and accomplish the mission. It takes courage to put the mission first, tackle personnel issues, and make hard decisions with lasting consequences. Serving in a leadership position requires assessing personal fear and using calculated courage the same as anyone else, but an effective leader must also acknowledge their subordinates' fears and help them overcome it. Leaders who account for and mitigate their subordinates' fears will gain the necessary trust and confidence required to excel in any environment. Leaders must understand the implications decisions, assignments, and unusual occurrences have on personnel. Three ways leaders can help others overcome fear are empathy, enthusiasm, and preparation.

Empathy

During the buildup to the siege of Fallujah in November 2004, Alpha Company was tasked with securing a large ammunition storage site well north of Fallujah. The objective was a compound in rural Iraq that stored munitions during Saddam Hussein's reign.

Intelligence reported the site was now occupied by insurgents and being used as an improvised explosive device (IED) factory. During the operation briefing, our company commander explained our scheme of maneuver and actions on the objective. The company would move to the objective in the early morning hours, surround the compound, observe enemy activity, and if needed, conduct an assault at daylight.

After the briefing, each element made final preparations for the mission: weapons maintenance, rehearsals, chow, etc. While final preparations were taking place and the sun was beginning to set, suddenly there was commotion in the company staging area. Everyone was called back together where we had had the briefing. The company commander told us the plan had changed. In a direct and excited tone, he asked, "What's our battalion's motto?"

Someone from the back yelled, "Victory to the bold, sir!"

The company commander replied, "That's right, victory to the bold! We are not going to cordon the objective off tonight and wait until morning. We are going to drive straight through the main gate tonight, and if they want to fight, we'll fight!"

The company commander's change of plans was instantly met with approval expressed by marines' shouts of "Get some!" "Rah," and "Kill!"

Most of the company left the second briefing excited about the aggressive change in plans, but not me. I knew I would be the lead vehicle. My crew was going to be the first to pass through the main gate and into the objective area, where intelligence had reported enemy contact as *likely*. I knew if the compound was defended, the main approach would almost certainly be covered by automatic weapon fire, IEDs, and obstacles. My crew would be responsible for punching through any initial resistance to prevent following units from bottlenecking and allow them to enter the objective area to assist.

The change in plans had serious implications for us; there was a disproportionate amount of risk for us compared to the units following behind. There was no issue with the plan; personally, I liked the new plan. We are marines; we'll go wherever and whenever you tell us to. But the unit leadership simply acknowledging the increased risk to my crew and offering understanding, support, and guidance would have made all the difference in the world. Leaders who make the effort, take the time, and empathize with subordinates gain perspective and put themselves in a much better position to lead and influence actions taken.

Enthusiasm

As stated in chapter 6, leaders are made. But some people are born with inherent traits, making the leadership development process easier. Of the many desirable traits of a high-functioning leader, enthusiasm is at the top of the list. Often overlooked, enthusiasm is essential for inspiring people to action. Enthusiasm is responsible for the inspirational charisma that draws people in, motivates them, and creates belief in a shared vision. The importance of enthusiasm is evident whenever observing peer-to-peer leadership where no positional authority exists. Just watch a Little League baseball game for a few innings and the informal leaders are easily identified, not because of their uniform insignia or title but because of their influence on their teammates and almost always because of their level of enthusiasm.

In early November 2004, we were gearing up for the impending siege on Fallujah. The day before we were scheduled to occupy our blocking position on the southeast side of Fallujah, we were offered a "warrior's dinner" at the chow hall on Camp Baharia. The chow hall was rudimentary and fashioned from a large green tent with a dirt floor and stuffed with folding tables and chairs. Though nothing fancy, it provided a warm meal that was not a Meal Ready-to-Eat (MRE) or tray ration (T-rat). While walking to the chow hall to partake in our ceremonial steak dinner, we noticed two MH-6M Little Bird helicopters making their approach to Camp Baharia. The Little Birds were new to us and not part of marine corps inventory. The passengers were hanging out the sides of the helicopters, resting their feet on the skids. They were some burly-looking dudes. In 2004, it was uncommon to see active-duty soldiers or marines with beards, long hair, and pieced-together uniforms of issued utilities, sneakers, and a favored college team ball cap. These guys were OGs. They were way out of regulations and did not care. We could tell they were professional, elite soldiers.

The Little Birds landed, and we continued to the chow hall. We got our thin steak with a side of green beans on a paper plate, sat down, and started eating. It was a somber dinner. There were marines from several different units who would be on the front lines fighting it out inside the city in days. Everyone was much quieter than usual, no customary ball busting and laughter that had become the norm, just everyone doing their best to enjoy the hot meal with the inevitable attack weighing heavy on their minds.

About halfway through dinner, the passengers who landed on the Little Birds entered the chow hall, grabbed plates, and found spots to sit and eat. Their presence was known to all the marines in the chow hall. They must have felt hundreds of quick glances in their direction. They were likely members of the army's elite Delta Force, and the marine infantrymen in the chow hall were all, a little starstruck, me included.

The Delta Team ate fast, policed their area, and began to exit the chow hall. But before they left, they took the time to acknowledge the marines in the chow hall that night. They made the rounds to every table, shaking hands, fist-bumping, backslapping, and pointing to those they could not reach. One shook my hand, nearly crushing it, saying, "I'll see you in the city, brother!"

After a few minutes, they exited the chow hall, hopped on the skids of their Little Bird helicopters, and left. A quick visit but a lasting impression. The entire mood in the chow hall had changed. A somber and quiet steak dinner filled with tension was now back to the usual ball busting and laughter. The enthusiasm of the Delta Operators was contagious. Completely spontaneous and certainly not required, the behavior of the Delta Team members is still one of the finest examples of leadership I have ever witnessed.

Preparation

The third way leaders help subordinates overcome their fear and perform when the stakes are high is with mental and physical preparation. As discussed, fear is both physical and emotional. Both types of fear can be greatly mitigated by/through a structured training process. Leaders must simply look ahead and anticipate the mental and physical challenges their people will likely encounter during their efforts to accomplish the mission. Highly effective leaders take this process seriously and ensure their people have the skills and mindset to confidently perform all tasks involved.

Leaders who invest in their people will always outperform those who invest in themselves. Fortunately, I learned this lesson early in my career when I was promoted to sergeant, a rank I revered because some of the most influential people in my life at that point had held the same rank while mentoring me. The short ceremony ended, and what was left of a platoon formation remained in the asphalt parking lot as I was congratulated by members of my platoon.

As things subsided and marines began returning to their duties, my platoon sergeant called me to his office. I jogged across the parking lot and entered the building to meet with him. I was ecstatic to finally be a sergeant, fully anticipating a big congratulations from the platoon sergeant and an initial counseling outlining new expectations. I shut the door behind me, turned to continue into the office, and was immediately met by the platoon sergeant in the hallway, who punched me in the stomach harder than I had ever been punched before! I doubled over; the wind was completely knocked out of me. I tried to stand upright, but that made the pain worse. A few seconds passed, and the platoon sergeant helped me upright by grabbing the collar of my utility blouse and forcing my torso vertical. In a yelling whisper, he said, "It's not about you anymore. It's about your marines. Now I look at them, if they are f——— up, then I know you are f——— up! Take care of your marines and they will take care of you!" Then he let go of my collar, pushed me away, and told me to get the f——— out.

The effects of the punch only lasted a minute or two, but the advice was life-changing and still applies today. It was a tough leadership lesson from a tough marine whom I am thankful for. "Take care of your marines and they will take care of you" does not mean coddling or sugarcoating. Taking care of your marines, subordinates, employees, or teammates means making every effort to ensure they possess the tangible and intangible skills required to succeed.

Effective leaders equip subordinates to mitigate physical fear through the relentless pursuit of perfection during realistic training. Training should be structured directly around the anticipated assignment and provide solutions for all likely and some unlikely contingencies. Training scenarios, workshops, and rehearsals conducted prior to execution should cover all implied tasks from the start to finish of the entire project. The lead-up and endgame are often overlooked during preparation but just as important as the main effort.

The work required to overcome physical fear brought on by stress can be a grueling process. Repetition after repetition must be mandated, observed, and critiqued until an overtrained response becomes so engrained that the body's physiological response to fear, known as "fight or flight," becomes just another day at the office. This level of proficiency transforms physical fear into a heightened level of confidence and capability.

Leadership also directly influences personnel toward courage through culture. Culture is king in any environment. Culture is responsible for the effort and productivity that go above and beyond. Legacy, tradition, and reputation are all represented in an organization's culture. People may join the marines for a paycheck or free college, but that is not what they fight for. Marines will fight tooth and nail and to the death if needed because of the marines who have gone before them, "such as regiments hand down forever."

Marines endure because their ancestors endured and expect no less—heroic and legendary marines like Dan Daly, Chesty Puller, John Basilone, and more recently, Cpl. Jonathan Yale and LCpl. Jordan Haerter, who stood their ground as a suicide bomber with two thousand pounds of explosives in a truck barreled toward their guard post. Yale and Haerter never wavered. They stood their ground, leaned into their rifles, and fired, shattering the truck windshield and the body of the coward driving the truck. The truck stopped short of its intended target and exploded, killing both marines but saving hundreds. These two marines displayed more courage in six seconds than most people will ever experience or could even comprehend. That level of courage and commitment comes from hundreds of years of heroic legacy and tradition instilled through structured preparation. Every organization has a legacy; every organization has a sacrifice. It just has to be identified and communicated to all levels.

Leadership is accountable for performance at all levels. To maximize performance, effective leaders must mentally and physically prepare their subordinates to acknowledge then overcome the fear holding them back. The fear that can consume someone on the battlefield is the same fear that keeps someone from going for a jog, putting in for a promotion, asking for help, getting sober, or even looking someone in the eye. But with awareness, recognition, and practice, fears become strengths, and both capability and confidence soar. Leaders and managers who acknowledge and formalize this professional-development process will increase the confidence and capability of subordinates and far outpace any competition.

Chapter 4

Develop Your Craft

Alpha Company received intelligence that a father and son living in our area of operations were directly supporting insurgent activity and building improvised explosive devices (IEDs). IEDs were the deadliest threat to US forces in Iraq during the fall of 2004 and responsible for multiple casualties within Alpha Company. We received a mission briefing at our company headquarters located just across the Euphrates River from Fallujah. The intelligence report identified probable locations where the father and son were located, and we were tasked with capturing or killing them. The platoon was organized into squad-size elements with ten to twelve marines per squad, then each squad was assigned a target building to assault. We would leave the overwhelming firepower of our armored vehicles behind and conduct the midnight raid on foot.

After the mission briefing, we rehearsed, inspected our equipment, and worked through possible scenarios. This mission was different. This was direct action targeting known insurgents and contrasted with the typical security and stability operations we had grown accustomed to. There was a unique energy and nervousness radiating from the marines, myself included. In these moments, hours feel like minutes, and minutes feel like seconds, and the inevitable soon happens, and it's time for action. All nonessential gear were stripped to travel light, remain silent, and move as quickly as possible.

The squad I was leading piled into the back of an armored vehicle. We would be driven to a preestablished release point, exit the vehicles, patrol to the objective, and assault our target building. The vehicle was a mortar variant of a LAV-25. Unlike traditional LAV-25s, these vehicles have no turret and are open in the back, serving as a makeshift personnel carrier when empty. The night was cold and dark; visibility was almost zero inside the vehicle. I felt around and found an object that provided the resemblance of a seat, similar to a milk crate. Once inside, we took a head count. I gave the vehicle commander the thumbs up, and we departed toward our objective.

As we began to move, I could hear a sound coming from the crate I had chosen as a seat. With every bump or turn, the sound of faint wind chimes would chatter below me. Eventually, curiosity got the best of me, and I used a red lens flashlight to illuminate the crate's contents. All I could do was laugh when I saw that what I had chosen as a seat was actually a crate of eighty-one-millimeter mortars. I thought to myself, "At least it will be quick, and good thing there's a dog tag in my boot!" The marine next to me also saw the sharp points of the mortars pointing at my ass, and we grinned and shrugged at each other as I turned off the light.

The LAV mortar variant slowed, and the vehicle commander gave the signal that we were approaching the release point. We stopped and exited as quickly and quietly as possible. Another quick count, and we headed out on foot to the objective area consisting of several buildings located inside a compound with a perimeter wall and gate. Many families in Iraq live in compounds with multiple small houses inside a perimeter wall or fence. Fortunately, the metal gate securing the compound was not locked, and we quietly entered. Familiar with the layout from the terrain model used during the mission briefing, we moved quietly but with a purpose to our target building and stacked on the front door, one behind the other. Our training taught us when the last marine is in place, he signals by squeezing the shoulder of the marine in front of him, silently notifying he's ready. The shoulder squeeze continues forward to the senior man usually positioned second from the door.

On this night, I was the senior man and felt the squeeze from the marine behind me. This was the point of no return, the moment of execution that determines if the preparation leading up to this moment was adequate or insufficient. The realization comes in the form of either fear or confidence when you get the squeeze. I felt confidence, took a deep breath in through my nose and out my mouth, visualized my actions passing through the threshold, and squeezed our point man. Instantly, the calm silence of a cold, dark night in Iraq was shattered as the front door was breached.

Developing your craft is an extreme form of preparation. A former company commander of mine, John Griffin, who now owns a business consulting firm, said it best,

> Everyone does their best during execution; that's
> a given but not good enough. Doing your best is
> about every moment that leads up to execution.
> Then your best will be good enough.

Successful leaders must be able to perform when the time comes. The saying "Fake it till you make it" does not apply to critical situations when the stakes are high and the pressure is on. Success is determined by the amount and type of preparation conducted prior to execution. Succeeding at a high level requires committing to the process of becoming an expert in your chosen profession. The level of knowledge and meticulousness required of a master sculpture or painter should in no way differ from the level of knowledge and meticulousness required of an infantryman clearing a building or a business executive conducting a sales presentation or the athlete seeking greatness. Developing your craft is treating your job as an art form and relentlessly pursuing the creation of a masterpiece when it's time to execute.

The importance of preparation is no secret. More than two-thousand years ago, the ancient Greek poet Archilochus wrote, "We don't rise to the level of our expectations. We fall to the level of our training." Proper preparation requires a deliberate process that is well thought out, comprehensive, and has clearly defined objectives. Simply stated, developing your craft requires a solid plan. Two categories drive the planning process. Because preparation cannot take place *after* execution, proper preparation considers (1) what is necessary during execution (tangible) and (2) what is required for sustainment after execution (intangible).

Tangible preparation is developing the knowledge, skills, and ability to master tasks necessary during execution. These are the physical tasks that are developed and practiced until an elite level of proficiency is achieved then maintained. This is the difference between good and great and one of the most common mistakes people make when evaluating their own proficiency level. I've seen it in the military, law enforcement, sports. It's everywhere if you know what to look for. A person gets a new piece of equipment or learns a new technique; they get a few repetitions, maybe practice for a few weeks, and they say to themselves, "I'm good. I got this," and they move on. They think they are proficient. What I say to them is, "Can you do it in the dark, in the pouring-down rain, standing on one leg while you are getting shot at?"

Developing your craft takes time, a long time, and to shine under the lights, you have to do the work in the dark. The process is the grind that goes on behind the scenes where no one is watching. Usually, people only see the finished product. Examples are the hotshot CEO or celebrity who bursts on scene or the athlete labeled the next phenom all described as "incredibly talented" or "overnight sensations." What doesn't make the headlines is the incredible amount of work and years of sacrifice it took them developing their craft prior to the recognition. No doubt these people are talented and probably sensational, but it didn't happen overnight.

There is no shortage of talented people walking the earth. What is rare is a talented person who is willing to put in the required amount of time and effort to do something extraordinary. It's rare because the process of developing your craft is not pretty; its hard work, often grueling work, done alone in the dark without compensation or recognition. Talent is overrated and talent by itself is common. Legendary baseball coach Ron Washington was once asked about his approach to coaching, and he said, "It's about repetition.

Give them reps until fielding a ball is as easy as pointing their finger." Next time you see a major league shortstop make a tough play look routine, it's because it is his routine. He's done it countless times—when he didn't want to, when he was hurt or tired—and he did it for free when no one was watching.

Success is never guaranteed, especially in the fluid environment. Intangible preparation is dedicated to the proper mindset to continue operating at an acceptable level until the mission is accomplished. Far too often, preparation solely focuses on the tangible requirements of performing the mission and completely neglects developing the mental endurance, resiliency, and resolve necessary to sustain efforts and finish strong. There must be an understanding that obstacles will be encountered, setbacks happen, and plans change. Proper preparation requires redundancy and contingencies during execution. Adversity is to be expected and planned for.

The planning process for developing your craft is the same on the organizational level as the personal level. While the organizational level will likely consist of several smaller plans combined to form one large all-encompassing plan, the process remains the same. Proper preparation involves the creation and maintenance of certain capabilities required for success. These capabilities are derived from known or likely scenarios anticipated during execution. Both tangible and intangible, these desired capabilities become the clearly defined objectives that measure progress, build proficiency, and eventually lead to success. The preparation plan becomes a road map to readiness that requires steps along the way that build and maintain capabilities.

Prior to deploying to Fallujah in the summer of 2004, my company completed a rigorous preparation plan. For six months, we trained on weapons, tactics, urban combat, and we conducted field training exercises. The tempo of the *workup,* as we called it, often outpaced actual combat. A few of us were given the opportunity to attend a special school in Riverside, California, that focused on security and stability operations. We were taught valuable lessons and new techniques from experienced members of the British Royal Marines, Australian special forces, the CIA, and other agencies. This knowledge was brought back and shared with every member of Alpha Company. A marine corps deployment workup is the equivalent of a preflight checklist that checks all the necessary boxes to ensure proficiency and operational readiness when a unit goes into harm's way.

All preparation plans will vary, depending on the chosen profession. Every discipline will have certain capabilities that are valued more than others. The skills required of a master cobbler vary drastically with the skills required of a rifleman, but for someone aspiring to be a successful leader, there are certain universal capabilities that should be developed. It is important to note that you must know the job thoroughly and possess a wide field of knowledge before you can lead. Below are five universal leadership capabilities that should be developed by anyone aspiring to lead well.

1. *Be physically fit.* The overall health benefits of being physically fit are obvious and should be enough to make physical fitness a priority for anyone. Proper diet and exercise lead to more energy, a sharper mind, and increased presence. In addition, rigorous physical exercise develops mental toughness and increases confidence in one's ability. Routine and demanding physical challenges create a familiarity with stressful situations. Become comfortable in uncomfortable situations! Consistently reaching your perceived physical threshold and finding the fortitude to take one more step or complete one more repetition reinforces that we are much more capable than we think we are and almost always limited only by our mental perception and attitude.

2. *Train in martial arts.* Closely aligned with the mental benefits of physical fitness are the benefits of training in martial arts. Brazilian jiujitsu, wrestling, and kickboxing are all very functional disciplines with real-world applications. Practicing martial arts increases confidence and discipline and improves cognitive function. The mental benefits gained directly result in a calm and capable command presence essential for a successful leader.

3. *Become technically and tactically proficient.* Successful leaders are masters at their craft. Knowing every aspect of a profession is a must to gain the trust and confidence of subordinates. Being tactically proficient means knowing how to employ technical knowledge in an appropriate and responsible way to accomplish the mission. Successful leaders know the job and understand how to strategically compete.

4. *Master public speaking.* Successful leaders are constantly giving presentations. Whether an impromptu session to guide or motivate a subordinate, delivering an operations order, or conducting a sales presentation, successful leaders must be confident and energetic when teaching, selling a product or service, or communicating their vision. Develop keynote speeches or presentations and practice them in the mirror or record them and critique yourself. Join a club or organization similar to Toastmasters and gain real-world experience. Watch and learn from talented public speakers and emulate what makes them effective.

5. *Be emotionally intelligent.* Emotional intelligence (EQ) is the ability to identify and manage personal emotions and the emotions of others. EQ is self-awareness, impulse control, empathy, and general people/social skills. The phrase "IQ gets you hired, EQ gets you promoted" is evident when observing successful and influential leaders. Emotional intelligence is a skill that can be developed, practiced, and improved over time. Viktor Frankl, Holocaust and concentration camp survivor chronicled his experience with emotional intelligence in his book, *Man's Search for Meaning.* Frankl stated, "Between stimulus and response there is a space. In that space is our power to choose our response. In our response lies our growth and our freedom."

You can't fake performance, and you can't fake physical and mental endurance. The time of execution is too late to get ready. Realizing that you are in your prep time and taking advantage of every opportunity to develop your craft is just as important as the execution. Use your prep time wisely and formulate a detailed plan on how, why, and what to prepare for. Do what is necessary now to sharpen your mind and body so that when you are the second guy in the stack and you get the squeeze, you feel confident and are not overwhelmed by fear.

Members of Alpha Company, Third Platoon, prepare for a night foot patrol. Left, Lt. Josh Phares; kneeling, Sgt. John Balcunas; right, Cpl. Martin Basso; center, Sgt. Barry Shaw (author)

Chapter 5

Decision-Making

In November 2004, Fallujah had been virtually abandoned by US Forces for six months. It had become a legitimate enemy stronghold and the epicenter of fighting in Iraq. In the spring of that year, as a result of increasing attacks against US Forces in and around Fallujah, the First Marine Expeditionary Force began offensive operations inside the city in an attempt to pacify it. The offensive, named Operation Vigilant Resolve and now commonly known as the First Battle of Fallujah, was triggered by a deadly ambush on four American private military contractors. The four men were killed, their bodies dragged through the streets, hung from a bridge, and burned. The incident made international headlines, and the images of insurgents celebrating while dragging American bodies through the streets demanded a response.

The First Battle of Fallujah lasted twenty-seven days with marines from the First Marine Expeditionary Force, making significant gains inside the city. However, American politicians couldn't stomach the nightly news footage of casualties and began a US withdrawal. After a month of hard fought gains by marines in Fallujah, the city was turned over to friendly Iraqi Forces in May 2004. The Iraqis had been trained and equipped by the United States and were tasked with finishing off the insurgency and maintaining security in a city that still had a significant enemy presence. This political intervention by way of premature transition of Fallujah to ill-prepared

Iraqi forces proved to be costly. The overmatched Iraqi forces quickly switched allegiance to the insurgents and either fled or joined the insurgency, taking up arms against US Forces.

After this strategic failure, Fallujah became increasingly dangerous. With minimal US presence inside the city, insurgents moved freely into and out of the city. Additional enemy combatants flocked to Fallujah, tightening their control within the city and surrounding area. By early fall of 2004, Fallujah had become such a stronghold that insurgents were bold enough to establish vehicle checkpoints inside Fallujah similar to US tactics. They were organized insurgents who spent the summer months fortifying the city in preparation for the inevitable US-led attack to reclaim the city.

With the insurgents left to do as they pleased, Fallujah was littered with IEDs, fortified fighting positions, and concealed escape routes. By the time our unit arrived in August of 2004, enemy fighting positions and bunkers hardened with sandbags and concrete were visible from the main highway that was skirting Fallujah to the east and north. Quickly realizing the transition of Fallujah to Iraqi Forces was a total failure, plans began to form for an all-out offensive to regain control of the city.

The little US activity I witnessed inside Fallujah were select marine recon units conducting Trojan horse missions to gather intelligence on insurgent activity. These units would dress like the locals and use an impounded car to drive deep into the heart of the city and document activities and terrain of strategic importance. These were the first marines I had ever seen with beards, and they were obviously nuts! Uniformed US personnel couldn't get within a kilometer of Fallujah without heavy armor and air support, but these marines went in with little to no support.

The only other presence inside Fallujah I saw was checkpoint 1. Checkpoint 1 was just inside where two major roads intersected on the east side of the city. The intersection of these two major highways made a large cloverleaf shape on a map and is how we referred to the area. Just west of the cloverleaf was checkpoint 1. It was manned by marines twenty-four hours a day, seven days a week, and checkpoint 1 was constantly engaged by insurgents. It likely served more of a psychological purpose than a strategic one. I believe it was a way of subtly informing insurgents that while they control the city now, with a couple tanks and a few marines, we can set up shop anywhere we want, and there's nothing they could do about it. I have the utmost respect for the marines of checkpoint 1. The mission they fulfilled was incredibly difficult and dangerous.

Around the first of November, the Light Armored Reconnaissance Company I was attached to (Alpha Company, Second LAR) was tasked with conducting an area recon just north of the city. Augmented with a tank platoon for security, we would be responsible for providing battlefield commanders with critical intelligence on selected locations for precombat staging and a large railroad berm that paralleled the northern edge of Fallujah. The railroad berm was significant because it presented a substantial obstacle for a US attack from the north while also offering some protection for US Forces as they staged.

We were briefed on the overall scheme of maneuver and the primary responsibilities for each section. Everyone knew their role in the operation. We also learned a high-ranking commander with experience as a tanker would act as a gunner in one of the tanks assigned to the mission, allowing him to have eyes on the terrain and obstacles, better preparing him for the planning process of the upcoming attack.

After linking up with the tank platoon and receiving final instructions, we moved to the north side of Fallujah using a raised roadbed to conceal our movement as long as possible. Eventually, each section broke off to conduct reconnaissance at their assigned locations. The tank platoon pushed closer to the city and provided security. We were traveling through rural terrain consisting of abandoned quarries north of Fallujah, moving independently to assigned ten-digit grids where specially trained scouts and engineers took pictures, which would later be collected and assembled to form a large terrain model of the attack positions and staging locations for the Second Battle of Fallujah's main offensive.

We systematically moved closer to the city, steadily working our way south toward the railroad berm, where scouts would exit the vehicle, take photographs, and measure the slope and width of the berm. As we progressed, we began taking indirect fire from insurgents inside Fallujah. Indirect fire in Iraq usually consisted of mortars and rockets. Our armored vehicles protected us from most of the razor-sharp superheated shrapnel sent flying in every direction upon impact, but a direct hit from a mortar or rocket would be catastrophic for an LAV.

We continued moving around the scattered quarries, gathering intelligence and documenting potential staging locations. After some time, we could tell the tanks were within range of the insurgents' direct fire weapons because of the level of fighting increased significantly. The tanks began receiving heavy small arms and machine gun fire and rocket-propelled grenades. A heavy firefight ensued.

As the recon element got closer to the city, the fire steadily increased. Most of the fire came from the Jolan District, thought to be the most dangerous area inside Fallujah. This reputation would be proven true a week later when the brave marines of Third Battalion, First Marines, assaulted directly into the Jolan District.

Soon, the LAVs were in range of direct-fire weapon systems, but the tanks were taking the brunt of it. Tanks have much heavier armor than an LAV and can withstand much more abuse. The tank's heavy main gun, a fifty-caliber machine gun, and powerful sights are devastating on the enemy.

With the area recon mission complete, it was time to make the last push to the railroad berm to measure its slope and width. This would allow commanders to determine if the berm could be traversed by US forces, or if it would have to be breached with explosive charges. There were significant concerns about closing the distance to the berm with the LAVs. They would most certainly encounter a hail of automatic weapons fire and rocket-propelled grenades on approach, and scouts measuring the slope and width of the berm would be exposed to heavy fire.

As we prepared for this part of the recon mission, we were alerted over the radio that one of the tanks had taken a direct hit from a rocket-propelled grenade. The RPG hit between the turret and the hull of the tank and had disabled its turret. The tank was still able to fight, but its ability to acquire and engage targets quickly was significantly reduced. Tanks are capable of delivering so much firepower on the battlefield that when one is damaged, the reduction in capability is felt immediately. Further, if an LAV or tank became disabled and lost the ability to move, the situation would become even more serious.

Taking everything into account—the damaged tank, increasing enemy fire, additional insurgents joining the fight for what they probably perceived as an attack, the thin skin of the LAVs, and marines expected to expose themselves to heavy fire while on the berm—the commander from RCT-1 made a bold decision and called in a Joint Tactical Air Strike Request. A JTAR called in fixed wing aircraft for immediate close air support for heavily engaged troops.

The commander also decided enough information about the terrain and railroad berm had been gathered to complete the mission at hand. Egress routes were quickly identified and plans made for the JTAR to suppress the enemy and cover the entire recon element's egress, thus limiting further damage and risk. Within minutes, two fast-moving fixed-wing aircraft screamed over our heads and dropped two five-hundred-pound bombs on the Jolan District. After that, every part of the recon element was able to safely move out of the area and return to base.

The area recon for the approaching battle's attack positions was a success. All gear and personnel were accounted for, critical intelligence was gathered on terrain and obstacles in the staging area, and everyone involved realized through experience the intense fighting that would be required to retake Fallujah.

Several takeaways related to leadership can be gained from the area reconnaissance mission. Leadership by example from the commander from RCT-1 was noted. The commander's decision to risk his own safety and comfort to experience the battlefield firsthand and put actual eyes on the terrain could be a book chapter alone. Also, the flexibility and coordination of several units working together to complete a very complicated mission under almost constant direct and indirect fire were significant and a direct result of the sound leadership involved in the planning process and execution. The primary leadership concept exemplified by this mission—it's complexity, execution, and success—is decision-making.

Decision making is a skill

Decisiveness and judgment have long been recognized as essential leadership traits, but they must stand together. Decisiveness coupled with poor judgment is a liability and good judgment without decisiveness is useless. Decision-making is a skill that can be taught and developed the same as any other skill. The following are proven methods that can be used to improve personal decision-making ability while developing the skills of current and future leaders. The commander from RCT-1's ability to quickly and accurately conduct a risk assessment in the midst of heavy fighting, modify the mission based on the calculated risk and desired end state, then act by requesting a JTAR showed his skill in decision-making. The commander's decisiveness and judgment accomplished the mission, protected marines and equipment, and killed the enemy.

Decision-making is an essential part of any leadership role. Every aspect of action in the workplace or in battle is a result of a decision or nondecision. Successful leaders don't consistently make bad decisions. Consistently making bad decisions leads to poor performance, inefficiency, reduced morale, and loss of trust. In the workplace, bad decision-making reduces profits and hinders growth. Poor decisions on the battlefield result in loss of life and mission failure. Immeasurable amount of time and research have been completed on how to improve the combat leader's decision-making ability. Combat leaders who can make good decisions quickly while engaged in a high-stress, rapidly changing environment are critical to success in battle. The same process combat leaders use to achieve victory in battle can be equally applied to any leadership role.

A successful leader will quickly determine one of the most important factors to consider when making a decision is the time available to make it. Time is critical and quite possibly the most important factor depending on the circumstances. It is important to assess the amount of time available when confronted with a decision. Some are time sensitive and may need to be decided immediately; others are not time sensitive and may benefit from a detailed planning process so an informed decision can be made. In both situations, waiting too long will lead to missed opportunities, slow operational tempo, and will eventually be viewed as indecisiveness. At the same time, making a decision too hastily could prove reckless and irresponsible.

There is a systematic approach for decision-making informed by combat, law enforcement, and private sector experience. This approach is first and foremost centered on the amount of time available and making the most of it. The more the process is used and developed, the more skilled one becomes at it. I rely on three different processes for systematic decision-making, each process determined by the amount of time available to make the decision. The three processes are as follows:

1. Immediate action
2. Decisions born from thought
3. Deliberate approach

High-risk scenarios capable of rapidly inflicting significant damage to personnel or the mission require the development of predetermined responses. These predetermined responses are known as immediate action drills to combat units. Immediate action drills are used when confronted with deadly situations without warning. Not having a predetermined response when confronted with an unanticipated high-risk problem can lead to being overwhelmed by the situation and an inability to make a decision or a decision that exacerbates the problem.

Immediate action drills exist for scenarios in combat such as ambushes, IED attacks, and sniper fire. Units train and rehearse immediate action drills so all members of the team are on the same page and can react immediately and appropriately when a scenario requiring a predetermined response is encountered. Successful leaders in combat or the workplace take on the responsibility of identifying possible scenarios that carry significant risk involved and require a decision to be made in the moment. Once identified, predetermined responses for these high-risk scenarios are developed, communicated, written down, and rehearsed. Immediate action drills become policies that limit high-risk areas and give personnel the confidence and ability to act quickly when a specific situation arises.

When a moderate amount of time is available, leaders can use a process termed "decisions born from thought." This process expands on the immediate action drill and is used when time is available for a problem or a problem is anticipated. Decisions born from thought is still a quick process but provides a systematic approach to make good decisions quickly, preventing decision paralysis.

The process of decisions born from thought was developed as a result of experience in high-pressure situations. Law enforcement can be much more complicated than combat. In law enforcement, there are too many scenarios to develop predetermined responses (immediate action drills) because no two situations will ever be alike. In combat, the mission, enemy, terrain, and time are almost always known, can be planned for, and likely scenarios anticipated and trained on.

The nature of law enforcement requires officers to make decisions in a constantly changing physical and societal environment. Every encounter a law enforcement officer has is different. Location, terrain, authority, purpose, capability, etc. are different for every single encounter. Law enforcement officers must develop the ability to determine an appropriate response based on what is about to occur or what is likely to occur. Law enforcement officers need the ability to operate with creativity, judgment, flexibility, and initiative. The same is true for the combat leader and the business executive, and a systematic approach to making expedient decisions born from thought is inherently better than a decision made from fear.

One example of an effective systematic approach for decision-making serves to empower officers to make decisions born from thought. The 20/20 Assessment PLAN is designed to provide law enforcement officers a format for developing their own custom immediate action drill prior to an anticipated situation or encounter. The process encourages creativity and good decisions based on available information and personal capabilities or limitations.

20/20 Assessment PLAN

Purpose

Know your purpose and authority prior to contact. Purpose and authority determine your level of awareness (white, yellow, orange, red).
White - Relaxed and unaware of what is going on around you. If attacked in condition white, you will probably die.
Yellow - Relaxed, but aware of who and what is around you to prevent from being totally surprised by the actions of another.
Orange- Something of interest has been identified that may or may not prove to be a threat. Remain focused until you are satisfied there is no threat.
Red - A threat has been identified and immediate appropriate action must be taken.

Location

Communicating your location and situation to dispatch and fellow officers prior to contact is essential officer safety.
- Always know your current location.
- Prior to any contact, notify dispatch of location, nature of stop, subject and vehicle/vessel information.
- "I will be out at Turkey point with two white males reference signal 68."

Anticipate

Determine the subject's most likely course of action and most dangerous course of action and have a predetermined response for both.
- By judging possibilities and probabilities, you can anticipate the subject's actions and plan accordingly.
- Develop simple, flexible plans for likely contingencies.
- Take initiative and deny the subject's ability to create an unsafe situation and cause harm to you or others.
- Having a plan increases speed of action and reduces surprise which can lead to shock and the inability to react appropriately. "A good plan executed now is better than a perfect plan executed too late or never"

Not
Today

Violent encounters are seldom lost by officers because they have been beaten, but almost always because the officer has decided in their own mind that they cannot win.
- Stay alert. Be vigilant. Never allow yourself to become a target of opportunity.
- Be prepared to face the challenge, believe strongly in your cause and NEVER QUIT.

The deliberate approach to decision-making is used for important decisions, usually strategic in nature, that determine the long-term direction and vision of an organization. Deliberate decision-making involves a meticulous approach using every resource available to make well-informed decisions that will have lasting consequences. This process is typically used by senior leadership within an organization when enough time exists to conduct a thorough and structured decision-making process.

The marine corps uses a six-step process known as the Six Troop Leading Steps. Commonly referred to as BAMCIS, an acronym which stands for Begin the Planning, Arrange Reconnaissance, Make Reconnaissance, Complete the Plan, Issue the Order, and Supervise. BAMCIS provides a model for deliberate decision-making that can be applied to any profession and easily modified and implemented for any situation.

Step 1, Begin the Planning. This is an information-gathering phase to gain an accurate estimate of the situation's size and scope. Every aspect of the situation should be analyzed to determine what the issues are, available resources, internal and external influences, potential impacts on the organization and personnel, and identify areas of potential concern and possible exploitation. The planning process is the most important step of the deliberate approach because it sets the course for the next steps. If the process moves forward based on inaccurate or inadequate information, the entire project could be jeopardized.

Step 2, Arrange Reconnaissance. In combat, this step is used to gather information on the enemy's capability, strengths and weaknesses, and applicable terrain. For deliberate decision-making, this step is used to identify issues, concerns, and information gaps identified during step 1.

Step 3, Make Reconnaissance. This is when leadership uses every available resource to fill information gaps and mitigate issues and concerns. In addition, one of the most beneficial things a leader can do when involved in the deliberate decision-making process is to gain a clear understanding of the situation by experiencing as much of the situation as possible. Known as a leader's recon, this is when the overall project manager and other key personnel gain firsthand knowledge of high-priority concerns. Information passed between multiple channels can become watered-down, contain personal interests, or just be inaccurate. Relying too much on second- or thirdhand information leaves the decision makers vulnerable to misinformation. When possible, leaders should make every effort to observe as much of the state of affairs as possible. This step was embodied by the commander from RCT-1 who chose to go into harm's way to have firsthand knowledge of the battlefield.

Step 4, Complete the Plan. This is when the decision is made. The plan contains a comprehensive understanding of the situation, a clearly defined objective, instructions on how the plan is to be executed, administrative and logistical needs, command structure, and communication protocols.

Step 5, Issue the Order. The method for issuing the order will vary depending on the size of the audience. For smaller audiences, in-person briefings are preferred, and for larger audiences, a written approach may be more practical. Technology has made it easier to address larger audiences using teleconferencing options to reach personnel in several different locations. Presentations should be followed up with written instructions that reinforce the presentation and contain appropriate visual aids. Effective communication is the most important aspect when issuing an order. Effective communication is ensuring that everyone involved is on the same page, down to the man.

Step 6, Supervise. The work does not stop after the decision has been made and the plan put into motion. Progress must constantly be monitored to ensure the objective is met in accordance with the plan. Leadership must verify efforts are in accordance with the plan and be available when problems arise.

In addition to developing and implementing effective decision-making processes, successful leaders have a responsibility to grow and improve the decision-making ability of their subordinates. Most decisions in both combat and business can be categorized as either tactical or strategic. Tactical decisions are typically made at the lower levels by leaders who are directly involved in the action.

Strategic decisions are made at the higher levels of an organization and should involve a deliberate and analytical process. First- and midlevel supervisors do most of the tactical decision-making.

In the military, these are noncommissioned officers and junior-level commissioned officers. These are the folks who get the job done while operating in a fluid environment. Tactical-level leaders have the most influence on productivity, efficiency, visibility, and morale for an organization. They likely base their decisions on past experience gained on the job or during training. This is not a bad thing, but it will likely limit the tactical leader's ability if they have limited experience or are confronted with a situation that cannot be solved by experience alone. In situations like this, the tactical leader should seek guidance from a supervisor.

However, providing guidance too often does not develop the decision-making ability of the tactical leader. A critical balance must be struck. Successful leaders provide the necessary tools to empower and encourage decision-making at the tactical level. An organization that produces tactical-level leaders capable of making sound and timely decisions independently will operate at a faster tempo than the competition and gain a significant advantage.

Developing strong tactical-level leaders is the key to unifying efforts within an organization. Tactical leaders must be empowered by upper-level leadership to make decisions. This involves increasing the tactical leaders' confidence in their ability and giving them the freedom to choose appropriate next steps within a clearly defined scope. Commander's intent is the most powerful tool a leader can implement to allow subordinates to exercise judgment and take initiative.

Providing the intent behind an assignment allows tactical-level leaders to continue making decisions in line with the desired outcome even if the initial assignment becomes irrelevant to the overall mission. For example: "Secure the two bridges located between Al-Karmah and Qaryat ash Shahabi in order to keep the main supply route open." Securing the two bridges is the task; keeping the main supply route open is the intent.

This was an actual assignment given to my Light Armored Reconnaissance Platoon during the Second Battle of Fallujah. If we had only been concerned with the assigned task, our unit would have completely neglected a larger bridge 1.5 kilometers north of Karmah. But because we knew the overall intent of the assignment was to keep the main supply route open, we secured the two bridges then aggressively conducted security patrols north of Karmah to protect the larger bridge. In the process, we discovered a daisy chain IED (two devices wired to detonate together) on the large bridge. Our engineers were able to successfully disable then destroy the IED, keeping all the bridges intact and allowing the main supply route to stay open. Guided by commander's intent, we were able to exercise initiative and confidently deviate from the original plan to accomplish the mission.

In addition to empowering subordinates through commander's intent, successful leaders must encourage decision-making by fostering an environment that promotes initiative and forward thinking. The famous management consultant Peter Drucker summed this up when he said, "Culture eats strategy for breakfast." An organization that does not support the development of its future leaders' ability to make sound and timely decisions will never reach optimal speed or efficiency. No policy, procedure, or strategy can take the place of a culture that values resourceful, talented, and dedicated people independently making decisions that align with the organization's vision.

Successful leaders must recognize that at the tactical level, decisions are made in a fluid and rapidly changing environment. The tactical-level supervisor may be under intense stress and working against a strict time constraint. In combat, at the tactical level, a perfect solution rarely exists, and tactical leaders must quickly choose the most promising course of action and focus on diligent execution. Far too often, lower-level supervisors and managers are scolded because of an outcome of a decision made while under difficult circumstances and limited information. This has a stifling effect on building a culture that encourages initiative and exercising judgment.

Leaders must use empathy when evaluating a subordinate's decision that produced a nondesirable outcome. A successful leader will spend more time evaluating their subordinate's intentions at the time the decision was made instead of focusing on the poor result. Using this process, supervisors and managers will likely come to understand why their subordinate made the decision they did and be able to use the situation as a teaching point.

Often, when evaluating intentions, mid- and upper-level leaders realize they themselves must accept some responsibility for the end result due to inadequate messaging or support. Evaluating intentions instead of results promotes creativity, develops judgment, builds confidence, and releases all the available talent within the organization.

Author pictured in the turret of an LAV-25. The green bridge where four American military contractors' mutilated bodies were hung and burned is in the background.

Chapter 6

Leaders Are Made

The first few days of November 2004 were busy around Fallujah. Everyone knew that an attack on the city was imminent, but the exact timeline was still a mystery to those who would do the fighting. The influx of equipment and personnel made it clear that zero hour was getting close. US psychological operations units were blasting messages to Fallujah residents, telling those who did not wish to fight to leave the city. There was a constant flow of war-making tools moving into the area. Tanks and artillery were packed inside Camp Baharia and Camp Fallujah. Seeing the amount of equipment and personnel assembling for the impending attack caused a deep tingling of fear and nervousness, masked by the dark and usually crude humor marine infantry units have come to master.

Final preparations were ordered, gear and personnel inspected, weapons and equipment checked then double-checked. An abundance of ammunition was issued, so much that it was hard to fit it all in the vehicle. No one wanted to run out of ammo! Every nook and cranny of the vehicles were stuffed with full magazines, fragmentation grenades, and ammo cans. An embedded reporter and cameraman were attached to the company to document our role in the approaching battle. Alpha Company's story would play out on nightly national news for a major television network.

Finally, orders came down: we would leave Camp Baharia a few days prior to the main attack and stage on the southeast side of the city. Instructed to prepare for approximately two weeks of sustained operations, we packed our bags, made our last phone calls to loved ones back home, and focused our attention on the tasks ahead.

I was a vehicle commander assigned to Alpha Company, Second Light Armored Reconnaissance Battalion and the lead vehicle for the four LAV-25s that made up Third, or Blue, Platoon. The call sign for my vehicle and crew was Blue 2. The lead vehicle is a position of prestige in a Light Armored Reconnaissance unit. Navigation, identifying location of threats, and likely the first to engage were added responsibilities for the lead vehicle. The crew could never let their guard down, constantly scanning for threats, keeping the rest of the platoon informed, and navigating through the war-torn area were demanding tasks accepted as an invisible badge of honor.

Soon after staging southeast of Fallujah, Third Platoon received its first mission providing security for a combat engineer section from Regimental Combat Team 1. The engineers were assigned to destroy several key bridges and roads and place obstacles south of Fallujah to restrict the movement of insurgents into and out of the city. The mission would take us much farther south than we had ever conducted operations.

The area south of Fallujah was known as the Zadon District and was notorious for being a dangerous area. The mostly rural district had little strategic importance in the grand scheme of Iraq operations. Lacking a substantial US presence, insurgent activity within the Zadon District was unchecked. We received our briefing and understood the mission, the route was identified, and graphics were updated on my map. I would lead the patrol to all the designated locations, our LAVs would provide security, and the RCT-1 engineers would place explosive charges on the roads and bridges and construct concertina wire obstacles, effectively sealing off the Zadon District from Fallujah, limiting the insurgents' ability to reinforce and resupply during the battle to come.

We stepped off on the patrol and began methodically making our way deeper into the Zadon District. It was an eerie feeling. We had operated enough in Iraq that we had developed the ability to observe a person working in a field, walking down a street, or driving a car and then subconsciously and almost instantly determine whether friend or foe.

We could tell from observing people in the Zadon District we were not welcome there. Some of the signs were obvious, some subtle, but all told us the same thing. Facial expressions were angry and perplexed to see a US-led patrol so deep in the Zadon. We completed the mission without incident, and several roads and bridges were destroyed or barricaded to cordon off Fallujah. There was a sense of relief following the mission. We had successfully conducted our first assignment directly related to the planned attack on Fallujah, now just days away, without incident. We returned to the company staging area on the southeast side of Fallujah and bedded down for the night, waiting to see what tomorrow would bring.

The relief felt from our successful first assignment was short-lived. The following day, we received orders to inspect every location where a road or bridge had been destroyed or an obstacle had been placed the previous day. If Iraqis had begun to rebuild any blown roads or bridges or tear down obstacles, we were to reestablish the obstacles. I was shocked by the assignment. Predictability is one of the greatest missteps in combat. Varying routes, times, and speed of patrols made it much more difficult for insurgents to pattern our behavior. The more random the activity, the more difficult it is for the enemy to identify behavior trends. If patterns or trends are observed, insurgents can formulate much more accurate and effective plans for inflicting damage and casualties. Variability when conducting security operations is a fundamental principle, and we were ordered to break it.

Immediately after the mission briefing, I approached the platoon sergeant for Third Platoon, Staff Sergeant Keisler. I voiced my concerns and did my best to encourage him to engage the chain of command and articulate the increased risk from retracing our exact steps from the previous day. I laid out options: the site could be inspected with air assets; we could complete the mission at night when our superior night vision capabilities provided an advantage. Staff Sergeant Keisler acknowledged he had the same concerns.

Frustrated, I broke protocol and approached our platoon commander, Lt. Josh Phares. Lieutenant Phares was very approachable and listened to his marines. A former college baseball player turned infantry platoon commander, Lieutenant Phares usually had more in common and seemed more comfortable with enlisted marines than other officers. These traits, along with many others, made him a very respected and admired platoon commander. I adamantly voiced my concerns to him about the assignment. Lieutenant Phares listened and agreed to consult the chain of command.

A short while later, he informed me the mission was still on but adjustments would be made to mitigate risk. The platoon was divided into two sections and augmented with additional assets. Half the assignment would be conducted with Third Platoon's Alpha Section, my and Lieutenant Phares's vehicles. Alpha Section would be augmented with a pair of LAV-25s, one operated by our company commander Capt. John Griffin (Black 6) and the other operated by a vehicle commander from headquarters platoon. Bravo Section consisted of Staff Sergeant Keisler's vehicle and Sergeant Palacio's vehicle and would be augmented with a platoon from First Reconnaissance Battalion. Splitting the patrol into two elements and augmenting with additional assets would make it more difficult for insurgents to pattern the patrol and provide much more firepower.

Alpha and Bravo Sections left the staging area and began verifying the obstacles placed the previous day remained adequate. As usual, I was the lead vehicle for Alpha Section. Even with the adjustments made to the patrol and the additional firepower, I was still concerned with the increased risk created by retracing our steps from the previous day. Now, restricted by our own obstacles, the route necessary to complete the mission was limited to a few options in and out.

Accepting the mission and the possible consequences, we made our way back into the Zadon District, checking off obstacles for our portion of the mission. Some obstacles had already begun to be repaired or removed by Iraqis, and we had to stop and take necessary actions to reestablish them. Bravo Section had similar issues, and the patrol began to drag out. Eventually, after we inspected and reestablished every obstacle, we were deep in the Zadon District and now had to get out.

With the primary mission completed, we turned north and began our trip back to the company staging area. Every tactic was used to vary the patrol's progress in an attempt to throw off plotting insurgents. We sped up, slowed down, and varied our dispersion between vehicles to remain as unpredictable as possible. Limited by our own obstacles, there was only so much that could be done.

Soon after our egress began, radio traffic began blasting over the net. The marine recon platoon attached to Bravo Section could be heard providing a contact report and telling their platoon's corpsman to get to the front of the Bravo Section column. Corpsman are navy field medics assigned to marine ground units. They provide lifesaving aid to wounded marines and are among the bravest on the battlefield. Marines affectionately refer to their corpsman as "Doc."

The lead vehicle of Bravo Section, Blue 4, had been struck by an IED. Looking to the south, I could see a faint cloud of smoke rising into the sky. The hectic radio traffic that followed was hard to listen to. Blue 4's vehicle commander was wounded, and we couldn't do anything about it. The marine recon platoon augmenting Bravo Section did an excellent job triaging injuries and coordinating a medevac. Blue 4's vehicle commander, Sergeant Palacio, had suffered overpressure injuries and shock and was transported to the trauma center at Camp Fallujah.

Alpha Section continued heading north, trying to reach the staging area before another attack could be carried out. I pushed the LAV to its max speed to be as difficult of a target as possible. Our driver, LCpl. Dan English, performed his job well. He took every precaution when operating the vehicle to protect the crew from IEDs and would eventually receive a Navy Achievement Medal with Combat "V" for valor, for his bravery and dependability during combat operations.

We were traveling north on a two-lane road with lush green farm fields on each side of us and approached a large man-made irrigation canal. The canal fed off the Euphrates River and provided farmers with water for their crops and livestock. A concrete bridge much like one would see on a two-lane road in the US was approximately two hundred meters ahead. The bridge was elevated just enough so the other side wasn't visible.

As we approached, a white vehicle appeared on the bridge traveling south directly toward us. At this time in Iraq, most civilian vehicles would pull over to the side of the road and allow approaching military convoys to pass. Military convoys traveled in the center of the road to add distance from the road's shoulder where most IEDs were located. Our first impression of the white car traveling south toward us was that it was larger than what was common in Iraq, and it was not slowing down or pulling over.

Lance Corporal English maintained his position in the center of the road. Our internal alarms sounded when the white car veered into the center of road, coming at us head-on. I jumped forward and unlocked the M240G machine gun mounted on the turret, but there was no time. The distance closed too fast. Knowing we were in great danger, I could do nothing to stop it. At the very last second, only feet from the front of our vehicle, the white car turned hard right and swerved around us. To this day, I remember the coward's tense face, eyes wide open looking straight forward, both arms locked out gripping the steering wheel.

I let go of the M240G and keyed the radio to alert Lieutenant Phares, the next vehicle in the four-LAV column behind us. As soon the radio keyed up, I was rocked by an explosion that blasted the back of my neck with superheated sand and dirt. The force propelled my torso forward on top of the LAV turret. My initial thought was, *They missed,* and thought a roadside IED had been detonated directly behind our vehicle prior to reaching the bridge.

Lance Corporal English started to slow down. I began gathering my wits and turned around to assess the damage. Lieutenant Phares's vehicle, Blue 1, was smoking and limping to the side of the road on flat tires. Believing the IED was much closer to our vehicle than his because of how powerful the blast had felt, I was confused by the damage to his vehicle.

The mental fog caused by the blast started to clear, and information began processing. There was a huge crater directly in the center of the asphalt behind Blue 1, much larger than a typical IED crater. There was no trace of the white car there just seconds ago. Then it hit me: we had encountered the most feared tactic used by insurgents in Iraq, a vehicle-borne improvised explosive device or VBIED. The only significant traces of the large white car that would be found were the engine block three hundred meters south of the crater and the license plate that somehow found its way inside Black 6's turret and miraculously caused no injuries.

I radioed to our company commander, "Black 6, this is Blue 2. Blue 1 has been hit by a VBIED. We are setting up security to the front." Black 6, Capt. John Griffin confirmed and coordinated security to the rear. We had to establish 360-degree security to protect ourselves in case of a follow-on attack while assessing the damage and treating the wounded. We chose the bridge because of the tactical advantage provided by its higher elevation.

While the scouts established a blocking position on the bridge, I turned to Blue 1 to see if there was any activity. Because of the magnitude of the blast, I was expecting the worst. The vehicle came to rest on the right shoulder. A moment passed, and I saw movement at the back of the vehicle: scouts were exiting and taking cover in a ditch next to the road. Counting marines as they exited, incredible relief increased with each marine: one, then two, then three, then four, until I finally reached seven! All seven marines were out of the vehicle and somewhat mobile.

It was obvious Lieutenant Phares got the worst of it. As a vehicle commander for a LAV-25, half your body is almost always exposed out of the top of the turret. Blue 1's scouts were applying field dressings to Lieutenant Phares's head, neck, and hands. He had suffered severe burns and lacerations. Not that anyone had ever questioned it before, but no one could ever question the toughness of Lieutenant Phares now. He had just taken a suicide car bomb to the chest and walked away.

We established a secure perimeter, and a medevac soon arrived in the form of our company first sergeant, Bryan Link. First Sergeant Link served as the senior enlisted advisor to the company commander and also acted as the vehicle commander for an LAV variant transformed into a medevac vehicle. First Sergeant Link would go on to conduct countless medevac operations in and around Fallujah, oftentimes putting himself at great risk to ensure his marines got the help they needed.

While he transported the wounded marines to Camp Fallujah's trauma center, Alpha Section maintained security on the blast site and was reinforced with a quick reaction force from First Reconnaissance Battalion. An explosive ordinance disposal team also visited the blast site and gathered intelligence on the size and type of VBIED.

Once everything was complete, we made our way to Camp Fallujah and linked up with the marines from Blue 1 and Blue 4 who had been medevaced. Lieutenant Phares and Sergeant Palacio would stay in the hospital and need a few weeks to recover. The others were released and cleared to return to duty. I will never forget the looks on the faces of some of the crew members and scouts from Blue 1 at the trauma center. It was a look of complete shock and bewilderment. I probably had the same look. The size of the blast was astounding.

The fact that the insurgent was the only person killed was nothing short of a miracle. Why that vehicle didn't detonate on myself and the crew of Blue 2 will never be known. Did the suicide bomber get cold feet? Did the bridge conceal our movement? Did our speed catch the suicide bomber off guard? At the last second, did the bomber think he could take out two vehicles? Regardless, everyone was alive. The vehicles, body armor, helmets, burn resistant clothing, etc. did their job, and the mental and physical toughness expected of America's marines was evident.

Third Platoon, minus Lieutenant Phares and Sergeant Palacio, eventually made its way back to the staging area as the sun started to set. A debrief was led by Captain Griffin, who also had been directly impacted by the events of the day. With the relative safety of the staging area and other marines now providing security, we could relax slightly and begin internally processing what had happened. We knew our journey was just beginning, and it was already shaping up to be wild ride.

The intensity of the situation was compounded for me when Staff Sergeant Keisler was designated as Third Platoon's commander, and I was reassigned as platoon sergeant. I went from being responsible for one vehicle and seven marines to four vehicles and twenty-eight marines on the eve of Operation Phantom Fury. In Sergeant Palacio's absence, Corporal Alvarado would move up from gunner to vehicle commander for Blue 4, Corporal Leal would become the vehicle commander for Blue 1, Cpl. Dave Echterling, a good friend of mine, would move from headquarters platoon and serve as the gunner on Blue 4. Five marines thrust into unexpected leadership roles by two IEDS just hours before the deadliest battle of the Iraq War. The following weeks would test our limits and push us far beyond our perceived capabilities.

For me, the few weeks following the VBIED would be the most challenging and significant experience of my life. Serving as platoon sergeant for Third Platoon during Operation Phantom Fury would result in a lifetime of leadership lessons and experience gained in a relatively short period of time. Sustained and fast-paced combat operations provide an unforgiving environment where mistakes are costly and not easily forgotten. The pressure, consequences, and intensity of the experience were humbling and at times overwhelming for a twenty-five-year-old. Looking back, what kept all of us grinding through constant adversity was knowing there were other marines and soldiers counting on us to do our jobs. Reflecting on both the experience and the process has made me certain that there are all types and levels of leaders, but successful leaders are made.

Becoming an effective leader is a process like any other skill. Leadership can be developed, practiced, honed, taught, and improved upon. While some people may naturally develop the inherent qualities of leadership, the bulk of what is necessary to become a successful leader can be intentionally learned by anybody. Anyone who is willing to dedicate themselves to the process of becoming a successful leader can do so with only two requirements: they must be determined and be willing to try and fail then try again with even more determination. For most people, this is the most important step to becoming a successful leader. Believing in one's personal ability to develop the necessary skills to lead successfully then committing to the process and adopting a positive attitude toward adversity is all that is required to get started.

Attitude is a critical factor. With each failure, someone determined to become a successful leader will learn, adjust, and courageously try again. The Bible encourages this process in the book of Romans: "but we also glory in our sufferings, because we know that suffering produces perseverance; perseverance, character; and character, hope." Leadership is a skill that will never be completely developed. No matter someone's experience or success, the possibility for improvement always exists. Obstacles, challenges, and failures never stop in a leadership position. The successful leader learns early on that these situations of adversity are opportunities for growth and development. Self-confidence coupled with commitment to the process is the first essential act to becoming a successful leader. The belief is the promise you can do it, the commitment is everything along the way that turns that promise into reality.

Leaders aren't made overnight. A *New York Times* bestseller, leadership conference, or motivational speaker does not suddenly transform someone into an effective leader. It takes time and effort. The process is the professional development of values that build the type of character people trust and respect. If the first step to becoming a successful leader is believing in one's ability, then committing to the process, the next step is beginning the professional development process by understanding the responsibilities of a leader and then identifying leadership qualities that support those responsibilities.

The responsibilities of a leader are taught to every marine during basic training. Success in battle requires sound leadership at all levels, and the marine corps takes this to the extreme. From day one, the professional-development process starts for entry level marines. While marine corps basic training is notorious for tough drill instructors blasting recruits with freshly shaved heads and instilling instant obedience to orders, there is also significant focus on developing the future leaders of the marine corps. The primary responsibility of marine leadership is mission accomplishment; the secondary responsibility is troop welfare.

Accomplish the mission—the number one priority on the battlefield. There is no confusion about what takes priority in battle. The mission comes before the safety of personnel. Fortunately, most leaders outside the military profession will never have to weigh accomplishing the mission against loss of life. However, putting the mission first is still the number one priority of a successful leader. No matter how smart, likeable, or respected a person in a leadership position is, if they fail to routinely accomplish the mission, they are not a successful leader. Prioritizing the mission first keeps everyone focused on achieving the ultimate goal. Whether victory in battle, on a ball field, or competitive market, the mission should always come first, and the priority of the mission should be known at the lowest levels of any organization.

After mission accomplishment, troop welfare is the second responsibility of a successful leader. Troop welfare, simply stated, is taking care of your people. Looking out for your employees' best interests, developing their talents, and providing proper equipment, resources, and training are all important aspects of troop welfare. Successful leaders set their subordinates up to succeed, support them along the way, and show appreciation for a job well done.

Successful leaders constantly try and balance mission accomplishment versus troop welfare. After making a decision that contributes to the success of the mission, an effective leader will immediately determine how the decision impacts personnel. If personnel will be impacted negatively, actions to mitigate consequences should be taken and reasoning behind the decision clearly messaged down the organizational structure. Successful leaders know and understand that putting the mission first may eventually require tough decisions adversely affecting employees. Success in these situations is reliant on the leader's vision being clearly communicated. Shared vision allows the impacted employees to look past any immediate consequences and focus on the long-term benefits of the actions taken.

Troop welfare does not mean coddling or enabling poor performance. Sometimes, troop welfare means initiating adversity on subordinates. On the battlefield, the number one aspect of troop welfare is keeping your people alive. It is difficult to repeatedly push people beyond their limits when they are mentally and physically exhausted. I've had disgust and anger directed toward me because of decisions I made during combat. It's not easy to deal with, but my intentions were always what I believed were in the best interest of my marines. Mandating hard work to improve our position, requiring extra rehearsals and equipment inspections, or increasing the volume and duration of patrols can seem antitroop welfare on the surface. In reality, all those decisions increased the long-term safety of those involved.

The same holds true in the private sector. Sometimes, leaders must weather a storm or two in order to secure long-term victories for your employees. This line of thought closely aligns with the Native American proverb, "Prepare the child for the path, not the path for the child." Occasionally, tough love can be the ultimate form of troop welfare.

In addition to mission accomplishment and troop welfare, an additional responsibility of a leader is appropriately managing resources. Successful leaders are both influencers and managers. Managing requires forward thinking to ensure adequate resources are requisitioned and maintained so operations can continue. Budget constraints, personnel matters, legal issues, and current events must all be taken into consideration during the planning and managing process to ensure sustainability of operations. Leaders must manage resources efficiently and exercise sound judgment to avoid becoming reckless. Recklessness will hinder mission accomplishment and may lead to unnecessary hardships on personnel.

Once the responsibilities of a leader are understood, aspiring leaders must learn, adopt, and develop the necessary leadership qualities that support and contribute to those responsibilities. These traits, values, principles, and beliefs will make someone an effective leader and capable of inspiring people to action. Deliberately identifying and adopting sound leadership qualities enable leaders to stay anchored in their core beliefs during challenging situations. Being deliberate in this process means taking the time to write down what leadership qualities are valued and why those qualities are essential to succeed in a leadership role. This process also serves as a personal contract to stay committed to those leadership qualities moving forward.

Below are some of the leadership qualities I value and use to guide my actions and support the responsibilities of a leadership position.

Integrity—the consistent practice of honesty, trustworthiness, and adherence to a strong set of values. Practicing integrity establishes and builds trust; trust instills loyalty; loyalty creates commitment translating into results. Successful leaders practice integrity both inwardly and outwardly, being true to one's self, coworkers, and the mission.

Vision—the ability and willingness to look ahead and anticipate future needs, problems, and actions of competitors and implement imaginative and creative solutions and tactics that mitigate foreseen hardships. Vision is offensive in nature and allows circumstances surrounding identified issues to be planned for and resolved prior to fruition. Vision allows leaders to shape and influence a future environment better suited for their cause. Successful leaders use vision as a strategic tool to help their organization gain the initiative over competitors, control operational tempo, and maintain momentum.

Personal Growth—Avoid complacency and strive to improve in all aspects of the chosen profession. Constantly self-evaluate known strengths and weaknesses; maintain and exploit strengths; commit to improving weaknesses. Remain humble and open to criticism. Listening and receiving constructive criticism are signs of strength and two of the most valuable learning tools.

Enthusiasm—possibly the most powerful factor for inspiring and motivating people to action. Belief in the mission is vital to genuine enthusiasm, so do something worth doing, and do it well! Enthusiasm is contagious and capable of spreading up and down the organizational structure. Successful leaders exhibit an inspirational charisma and passionately sell their vision and direction to create a strong sense of purpose within employees.

I was able to participate in the marine corps professional development process and learn and develop sound leadership practices in the classroom, on the job, and in battle. I have also been fortunate to have been led and influenced by exemplary leaders throughout my career. These leaders inspired me to achieve much more than I ever thought possible. I learned from their example and emulated their dedication and purpose. To this day, I still rely on the example and standards of the leadership provided by Lt. Josh Phares, Capt. John Griffin, 1SG Bryan Link, and many others. I witnessed and interpreted their leadership as unwavering courage with an incredible sense of purpose and dedication to the mission and to their marines. Many times, I doubted my own ability but persevered because of the expectations of successful leaders I genuinely respected.

The aftermath of a suicide car bomb in the Zadon District south of Fallujah. Blue 1, Lieutenant Phares's vehicle is seen resting on the shoulder of the road with the back hatches open.

Chapter 7

Shoot, Move, Communicate

On November 7, 2004, I woke up on the ground under a light armored vehicle in our company staging area southeast of Fallujah, still trying to process the events of the day before when a suicide car bomb detonated in our column of vehicles. The bomb wounded our platoon commander, Lieutenant Phares, whose vehicle absorbed most of the blast. A separate roadside bomb injured another vehicle commander from our platoon during the same operation. The two IED attacks occurred within an hour of each other. As a result, our platoon sergeant, Staff Sergeant Keisler, took over for Lieutenant Phares, and I assumed the duties of platoon sergeant.

On the eve of the Battle of Fallujah, I went from being responsible for one vehicle and seven marines to four vehicles and twenty-eight marines. With the morning, the shock of the events on November 6 began to fade as they became overshadowed with the heavy weight of increased responsibility and the knowledge that our toughest days were still to come.

Alpha Company was tasked with maintaining the perimeter for a portion of Fallujah called Queens. Two platoons rotated twelve-hour shifts and deployed along a two-kilometer area to ensure no insurgents escaped and engage enemy targets according to the rules of engagement. The perimeter was completed by a marine recon battalion directly south of Queens and the Euphrates River immediately to the west, covered by a company from Third Light Armored

Reconnaissance Battalion. The upcoming attack would come from the north, forcing insurgents to fight and die, surrender, or flee into the marine units forming the perimeter. The city was essentially sealed off. There was no escape and no way possible for the insurgents to receive reinforcements or resupply.

As the hours passed, the anticipation of the attack increased. Finally the time came. We received our final briefings, moved from the assembly area, and took our positions. My vehicle was the farthest to the north with four additional vehicles spread to the south, linking up and mutually supporting marine recon units farther south. The two-kilometer stretch we were responsible for was open terrain with a few structures and a minefield between the perimeter and the city. The terrain allowed us to cover a lot of ground with our thermal sights, the two-thousand-meter range of our twenty-five-millimeter main gun, and the four-thousand-meter range of the TOW missile LAV in our platoon. An interesting side note is that any Operation Phantom Fury map available on the Internet shows an army brigade combat team assigned to our portion of the perimeter. An army BCT consists of four thousand soldiers. The fact is this area was secured with a reinforced Marine Light Armored Reconnaissance Platoon of thirty-two marines just before midnight.

The battle started just before midnight. A curtain of artillery shells exploding over buildings on the northern edge of the city appeared. It was the equivalent to an epic fireworks grand finale that lasted all night and was five kilometers long. The difference was these fireworks were coming down and exploding downward onto insurgent positions. The amount of ordinance dropped on the city created a white sparkling cascade steadily flowing downward onto rooftops, alleyways, and streets inside Fallujah. This relentless onslaught was only interrupted to inflict more damage on the city.

Occasionally, as if someone flipped a switch, everything stopped. The sky would go black and quiet. Then massive explosions could be seen and felt as planes zoomed overhead, sending large precision-guided bombs into known insurgent positions. Under the cover of darkness, these aircraft were invisible to the naked eye and only noticed by the damage they inflicted and the roaring of their engines heard moments after their assignment had been completed.

Witnessing the full force of the United States Military unleashed on a fortified city was an awe-inspiring experience. The magnitude, volume, and escalation of the attack are indescribable. Slowly, artillery began to inch south, allowing marines to enter the city and begin the vicious house-to-house fighting required to secure Fallujah. Tracers and secondary explosions a few hundred meters behind the wall of artillery was evidence that marines were inside the city.

Knowing marines were engaged in an all-out assault not far from our position brought mixed emotions. Knowing your fellow marines were fighting it out only a couple kilometers away and not able to do anything to help was one of the worst feelings I have ever experienced. All of us wanted to abandon our assignment, which seemed unnecessary at the moment, and join our brothers pushing into the city. But our mission was to secure the southeast side of the city so the main effort could focus on their assignment.

After watching the pounding the city had taken, it was astounding that there were any insurgents still alive with the will to fight. The scenario reminded me of books about marines assaulting Pacific beaches in World War II, when naval gunships would pound an island for days or even weeks prior to an amphibious assault and still be met with ferocious opposition.

As the assault continued, radio transmissions increased. We had two radios inside our light armored vehicle, which allowed us to communicate effectively and monitor the progress of adjacent units. Since my vehicle was positioned the farthest north, we programmed our second radio to monitor Regimental Combat Team 1's radio frequency. RCT-1's call sign was Inchon in recognition of the marines' amphibious landing and battle during the Korean War. RCT-1 was the headquarters element overseeing the attack on the city. Monitoring this radio frequency allowed us to track the lead elements of the assault, so when the time came, none of our fire would endanger our fellow marines and soldiers.

As the battle progressed, I positioned my vehicle three hundred meters south of our most forward unit and made sure no fires went north of my position. There was constant radio traffic over Inchon's net from battalion commanders and operations officers providing situation reports or requesting support for their marines waging war. Two of these still stand out.

The first was when a battalion operations officer hailed Inchon and reported that a marine had been confirmed as killed in action. To my knowledge, this was the first marine killed during the battle. The marine had been shot while clearing a house. Following the KIA report, the operations officer informed Inchon that while one marine was KIA, four insurgents were killed in the exchange. The kill ratio seemed to be of importance to the command element. This was a sobering moment to everyone who heard the report. What we were witnessing just became very real. That marine had a family, friends, a home, goals, and aspirations, and now he was dead.

The second radio transmission that still stands out came from one of the two C-130 gunships over the city providing fire support and engaging targets of opportunity. A C-130 pilot hailed Inchon:

C-130: Inchon, Eagle 1.
INCHON: Eagle 1, this is Inchon 3 [RCT-1 operation officer], go ahead.
C-130: Inchon, the vehicle-borne improvised explosive device [VBIED] threat inside Fallujah proper has been eliminated.
INCHON: Roger, Eagle 1.
INCHON: Eagle 1, this is Inchon 6 [RCT-1 commander]! Say again!
C-130: Roger, Inchon 6, the vehicle-borne improvised explosive device [VBIED] threat inside Fallujah proper has been eliminated.
INCHON: Eagle 1, how can you possibly verify every VBIED has been eliminated inside Fallujah proper?
C-130: Ah, roger...every vehicle inside Fallujah proper has been engaged.
INCHON: Roger.

The battle raged for days at the same intensity with which it began. The main effort continued to push south directly into and through the most hardened and heavily defended neighborhoods inside Fallujah. At one point the city was both flooding and burning at the same time. After three days of constant fighting, marine units reached their objective, and a mechanized army task force swept across the city from east to west, forcing remaining insurgents to the edge of the Euphrates River or Southern Fallujah. Insurgents who chose to flee to the west were met by marine units closely monitoring the Euphrates. Some insurgents attempted to escape by floating downriver using beach balls as makeshift rafts, making easy targets for the marines on the western perimeter.

As more insurgents were forced into the *Queens* section of Southern Fallujah, our platoon's tempo increased. Marine and army units continued to clear the city moving south, forcing insurgents deeper and deeper into Queens until the section was bursting at the seams. We began receiving persistent and accurate mortar fire. On one occasion, we were stationed on the southeast side of the city when a mortar landed two hundred meters behind our vehicle. A moment later, a second mortar landed one hundred meters to our front. It was obvious the enemy was bracketing us to determine an accurate range, and the next mortar was likely to drop right on top of us. I told my driver, Lance Corporal English, "Let's get out of here. Start the vehicle, and let's go."

About the same time the vehicle slipped into gear, I heard a very loud *shhh*, and then a puff of dust rose up ten meters in front of the vehicle. Time slowed way down. Seeing the puff of dust, I thought to myself, *I'll be damned. It was a dud.*

Then it exploded! The blast pushed me back against the turret, and the heat and sand from the explosion pounded my face. A little dazed and spitting the sand out of my mouth, I heard the radio key up. It was Staff Sergeant Keisler, the acting platoon commander, whose vehicle was only a couple hundred meters to the south. He saw the whole scene play out. "You okay?" he asked in a "holy shit" tone of voice.

All I could do was shake my head and reply, "Roger." We were okay. The armored vehicle had once again done its job and shielded us from danger, but we would be much more expedient in changing positions next time.

On the fifth day into the battle, we were still maintaining our position on the southeast side of Queens. Every day, we would move a little farther south, still positioning the vehicle on our right lateral limit as we faced the city. In the early afternoon, an army scout platoon linked up with us and began scanning the area with their powerful thermal sight. The forty-power sight mounted on top of the army Humvee was much more powerful than the fourteen-powered thermal sights outfitted on our armored vehicles. Almost immediately, the army scout team leader keyed the radio and informed us they had identified a dug-in insurgent sniper to our direct front. The army scout team leader described the building where the enemy sniper was lying in wait for the marines and soldiers approaching from the north.

Cpl. Adam "Ginger" McGing engaged the target with twenty-five-millimeter high explosive rounds from the turret-mounted Bushmaster chain gun. A couple of three-round bursts—*thump, thump, thump…thump, thump, thump*—and Ginger was putting deadly, accurate fire directly into the sniper's position. Additional LAV-25s began to fire, and the enemy position was soon covered with sharp white flashes as twenty-five-millimeter high explosive rounds traveling approximately 1,100 meters per second found their mark. Smoke began to climb into the sky, and secondary explosions could be seen in and around the enemy position. The army scout team leader continued to provide updates over the net, "Keep it up. You guys are all over them!"

The volume and accuracy of the fire was too much, and insurgents soon began fleeing the building to nearby structures. The army scout team leader with eyes on the target provided updates and identified additional targets. Ten to twelve insurgents were seen leaving the building. The ancient mud buildings provided the insurgents with excellent cover. It would take more than twenty-five-millimeter firepower to destroy their positions.

I requested fire support through our company executive officer and radioed the distance and direction. The first round was two hundred meters long. I relayed the correction, and the next round was right on top of the enemy position. I radioed, "Fire for effect."

Moments later, six 155-millimeter artillery rounds plunged into the buildings occupied by the insurgents. Large plumes of smoke drifted high into the sky as our twenty-five-millimeter rounds continued to smash into the insurgent positions.

As more secondary explosions and movement were observed in the area, I radioed to our company executive officer to repeat the previous fire mission. Six more 155-millimeter artillery rounds found their target. When the smoke cleared, the army scout team leader, momentarily losing his bearing, transmitted over the net, "You guys fucked them up!"

Success on the battlefield for any ground combat unit lies in the unit's ability to effectively shoot, move, and communicate. The phrase "shoot, move, communicate" is engrained into every ground combat soldier and marine. So much so, often times, when an infantryman is asked what they do, they will simply reply, "I shoot, move, and communicate." It sounds simple enough, but the ability to effectively perform the three functions as a unit on the fast-paced, violent, and constantly evolving battlefield is very difficult and requires preparation and sound leadership.

The tangible aspects of shoot, move, and communicate combine to form a mindset and culture that continuously strive to improve every situation. The concept does not allow for idle time. It encourages and mandates constant progress toward the objective. If you cannot move, then you shoot; if you cannot shoot, then you move; if you cannot communicate, you move and shoot until you find a way. Simple terms on the surface, shoot, move, communicate are actually very complex when examined closely. Understanding the complexities of each action makes the "shoot, move, and communicate" concept transcend any discipline and a requirement of an effective leader.

Shoot

Shoot, the simplified term for *engage*. The point when two opposing forces meet and action is required. The very essence of battle is summed up in the marine rifle squad's mission statement: "To locate, close with, and destroy the enemy using fire and maneuver." Engaging the enemy requires decisiveness, commitment, and courage from the unit leader. Combat leaders are responsible for their team's actions and accountable for the results those actions produce. Every shot fired has a consequence, good or bad. Leaders must ensure actions taken during an engagement are calculated, align with the mission, are in accordance with the rules of engagement, and minimize collateral damage. Shooting is not reckless destruction but targeted action that neutralizes immediate threats and mitigates risk.

Successful leaders take a proactive approach to identify high-risk areas of concern and encourage swift and precise action to mitigate or eliminate threats. Problems in the workplace cannot be ignored or allowed to grow and fester, compromising the mission. Can you imagine a combat leader observing the enemy preparing to attack and doing nothing? Combat forces action because life and death are at stake. Successful leadership in the workplace requires the same keen observation skills and targeted action to identify and neutralize threats to personnel issues, budget concerns, and high-risk business practices.

Move

There are two types of movement on the battlefield: tactical and strategic. Tactical movement is the act of moving from point A to point B in a manner that provides an advantage over the enemy. The two basic forms of tactical movement are "fire and movement" and "fire and maneuver." Each type moves toward an objective while providing observation and fire support for the element in motion.

Tactical movement is a skill developed through countless training hours rehearsing how to move and respond to threats as a team. The focus is on the effective use of the cover and concealment provided by the terrain while traveling toward the objective. In combat, whoever uses the angles offered by the terrain better and more often, while shooting accurately, will usually win. Tactical movement is gunfighting. Gunfighters are forward looking, disciplined, and calculated. Thinking like a gunfighter has value in any leadership position and is typically most valued and implemented at the lower levels within an organization.

Leadership positions at the mid and upper levels value and implement strategic movement. Strategic movement can take many different forms. It generates and exploits advantages over the competition. Strategic movement on the battlefield is the art of maneuver warfare, which is based on rapid, flexible, and opportunistic positioning to accomplish the mission as effectively as possible. Strategic movement happens at the higher levels, initiated during the planning process and constantly updated throughout the execution phase based on observations and anticipated reactions. Advantages to successful strategic movement are not only physical and positional but can be psychological, technological, and temporal as well.

Successful leaders understand the benefits of gaining strategic advantages across as many dimensions as possible. Focused efforts that exploit a competitor's vulnerabilities and market trends will generate and maintain momentum, forcing an operational tempo that eventually overwhelms the opposition. Leaders engaged at the strategic level must adapt and develop the necessary skills and traits necessary to operate in a fast-paced, constantly evolving, and uncertain environment. Flexibility, initiative, boldness, and the willingness and discipline to take full advantage of every opportunity are required to succeed at the strategic level. Strategic level leadership must also have the unique ability to operate and thrive independently while self-regulating personal satisfactions and ego, always maintaining the agency's mission as the overall priority.

Communicate

Communication is well known as one of the most important factors that contributes to success, efficiency, and morale. It is an attribute of virtually every successful leader. Any roundtable discussion or leadership seminar that addresses what is necessary for improvement will have communication listed as a priority for both individuals and organizations. Communication is one of the most discussed topics but also the most misunderstood. Most discussions on the need for improved communication close with everyone agreeing to communicate better, but nothing changes. I have personally been involved in countless discussions like this and left contemplating, "So…communication is important, but how are we going to communicate better?"

Communication is complicated and getting increasingly so as technology continues to advance. The speed at which information becomes available is a force to be reckoned with. E-mail, cell phones, social media, videoconferencing, and good, old-fashioned conversation make communicating both easy and complex.

To overcome the challenges and mystery surrounding how to communicate effectively, successful leaders must understand what effective communication is. Sustained combat operations are the ultimate proving ground. The tempo, friction, violence, and uncertainty associated with war make the easiest tasks difficult and difficult tasks seemingly impossible. The ability to communicate effectively is challenged during battle. Communication protocols and procedures will be tested and pushed beyond the breaking point, forcing leaders to act on little, outdated, or no information concerning the ever-changing situation. Leadership experience in this environment demystifies what effective communication is and reveals its simplicity. Effective communication occurs when everyone, down to the man, is on the same page. Successful leaders make every effort to ensure this is the only acceptable standard.

In the days leading up to the Battle of Fallujah, certain members of Alpha Company were invited to attend the operations brief for the all-out attack planned on Fallujah. Fortunately, I was included. This type of operations order was typically reserved for key leaders such as officers and senior enlisted, who would relay the information down their chain of command. Because of my role as the lead vehicle for the platoon and the company, I was asked to sit in.

At the briefing, I had never seen so many high-ranking officers in one place. There were generals, colonels, and battalion commanders who would lead their men straight into the fortified city. The briefing featured the largest terrain model I had ever seen. Terrain models provide a visual picture for those receiving the order, and this one must have taken weeks to build. I had a front-row seat to the official operations order for the Siege of Fallujah. Though I personally played a tiny role in the battle, after the briefing, I knew what that role was and why it was important.

That information became even more critical after my platoon commander Lieutenant Phares was wounded the day before the start of the battle. If I had not attended the briefing, much of the information would have left with Lieutenant Phares on the medevac.

Armed with knowledge of the big picture and the scheme of maneuver, I had a clear and concise understanding of our responsibility during the battle. I knew we had to closely regulate our fire to the north, monitor RCT-1's radio frequency, and track the assault's forward progress to prevent a friendly fire incident. I was aware there was a minefield between our position and the city, I understood the phases of the attack and could adjust our tactics to complement each phase, and I knew why our mission was important. Attending the briefing allowed me to be proactive, exercise initiative, take ownership of the mission, and find a way to contribute to the main effort.

Effective communication is equipping everyone with the same information from top to bottom. It provides vision, instills purpose, and creates ownership, resulting in unified action toward progress. In 1962, Pres. John F. Kennedy visited NASA to observe the work devoted to space exploration. While touring the facility, President Kennedy stopped a man carrying a broom in a hallway. The president asked the man what he did for NASA, and the janitor replied, "I'm helping to put a man on the moon." This is an example of effective communication. The janitor understood his role in support of the overall mission.

Successful leaders are directly responsible for ensuring information passes freely up and down the chain of command. Information is a weapon, a valuable tool that initiates action, maintains tempo, and forces precision. It is the reason the radio is still the primary communication device for military and law enforcement. Every transmission is heard by all involved. Successful leaders implement and mandate communication procedures that clearly communicate the who, what, where, when, why, and how down to the man!

Author's view returning to the Second Battle of
Fallujah after refueling and resupplying.

Author's view looking west down Route Michigan or Phase
Line Fran during the Second Battle of Fallujah.

Chapter 8

Commander's Intent

In November 2004, the Light Armored Reconnaissance Platoon I was assigned to was pulled from the inner cordon of Fallujah and reassigned to the small city of Karmah. The assignment came about a week after a suicide car bomber had swerved around my armored vehicle and detonated in front of our platoon commander's vehicle, seriously wounding him and causing our platoon's command structure to change. Staff Sergeant Keisler, our platoon sergeant, assumed the duties of platoon commander, and I was moved into the platoon sergeant role.

Since the blast, the platoon had been conducting operations in direct support of intense urban combat in and around Fallujah. At first, the added responsibility given to me on the eve of the Second Battle of Fallujah caused stress and concern. Going from being responsible for one vehicle and seven marines to four vehicles and twenty-eight marines was an unexpected burden during an already stressful time. But I quickly grew accustomed to the new and increased responsibilities as platoon sergeant because of the fast-paced operational tempo, and the platoon was functioning well.

The new assignment in Karmah came with a new challenge. The platoon would be detached from the company headquarters element and operating independently. Without the safety net of our company headquarters' presence and oversight, the increased responsibility of filling the platoon sergeant role felt heavy again. We were to relieve an army Stryker platoon and protect two strategic bridges on one of the main supply routes east of Fallujah. Positioned between two small towns, Qaryat ash Shahabi and Al-Karmah, were two bridges with strategic importance, necessary to keep the supply route open. If left unprotected, insurgents could easily destroy the bridges and restrict US movement around Fallujah. The bridges were about 150 meters apart with the city of Al-Karmah immediately to the north and Qaryat ash Shahabi immediately to the south.

Karmah was about ten kilometers east of Fallujah, and because virtually every resource had been dedicated to the city, where the fighting was still going strong, we would essentially be operating alone and completely self-reliant for the first part of the assignment. The mission mandated a constant presence at the bridges to ensure the supply route's integrity. We would live between the two small towns, constantly observed and tested by an active insurgency operating inside Karmah. The new assignment came late at night and was effective immediately. Our company commander, Capt. John Griffin, issued us the order. Captain Griffin explained the situation and told us what our mission was. "Move to this location, conduct a relief in place with the army Stryker platoon, and secure both strategic bridges in order to keep the main supply route open for friendly forces." Staff Sergeant Keisler and I understood the mission, issued subtasks to other members of the platoon, and prepared to move out.

We left the company staging area on the southeast side of Fallujah around midnight and traveled north to the intersection of Route Mobile and Michigan, known as the Cloverleaf. We exited on Route Michigan and traveled east for about ten kilometers. I was the lead vehicle of the four-vehicle column. This was new territory for us; until now, we had never operated in this area, so navigating the platoon in complete darkness was a challenging task. Navigation was conducted with a topographic map, compass, protractor, and a store-bought GPS.

We turned north off Route Michigan, continued toward Karmah, and soon arrived at the army Stryker platoon's position. We weaved through a makeshift entry control point (ECP) fashioned out of concertina wire and past a small car riddled with bullet holes. The car reeked of death and was the initial indicator that we may have some tough days ahead of us. Inside the perimeter, we dismounted and made contact with their platoon commander and platoon sergeant.

The army lieutenant and sergeant first class showed us their perimeter and filled us in on the enemy situation. They had six armored vehicles, known as Strykers, very similar to ours. The main supply route ran directly through the center of their position. ECPs were maintained on the north and south sides with the Strykers facing outward, providing overwatch for the ECPs. Soldiers occupied fighting positions at each ECP, and a sniper team was positioned on the third floor of an abandoned ice factory just north of the perimeter focused on Karmah. The army platoon was exhausted and wanted to leave the area quickly to get some rest and hot chow. They had endured heavy fighting and constant harassment while occupying the position we were about to take over.

Staff Sergeant Keisler and I had a dilemma on our hands. The army platoon was much larger than ours. They had more vehicles and personnel than we and had a four-person sniper team. There was no one to consult, no higher headquarters to ask advice from. We were the only ones with eyes on the terrain. It was a difficult area, a tactical nightmare for our relatively small unit. We had plenty of firepower, but the effectiveness of that firepower would be severely diminished in the urban environment where the enemy can easily close the distance. We were restricted to this exact location, surrounded by urban terrain and dead space, with two high-speed avenues of approach leading directly into our position and virtually no support.

Staff Sergeant Keisler and I discussed options. We had our orders from Captain Griffin. "Move to this location, conduct a relief in place with the army Stryker platoon, and secure both strategic bridges in order to keep the main supply route open for friendly forces." We were on location and ready to conduct the relief in place, but occupying the existing army positions would spread us too thin, putting the mission and the safety of our marines at risk. Our platoon was likely chosen for this assignment because our marine Light Armored Reconnaissance platoon was of similar size and capability as the army Stryker platoon. Firepowerwise, we probably had an advantage, but personnelwise, we were at a distinct disadvantage. At that moment, I would have traded two LAV-25s for a squad of marines.

A decision had to be made. We needed the security of the army platoon while we got set up, and the Strykers were ready to leave the area as soon as possible. The terrain, coupled with our platoon's capability, made a traditional relief in place impossible. One of the first decisions I made in my new role as platoon sergeant operating independently of the company was to deviate from the mission. As a young marine in an unexpected leadership role, deviating from the mission in any way was a big deal. The marine corps is an institution built on discipline. Instant willing obedience to all orders is the mantra during basic training. But while discipline is a necessary attribute for combat soldiers, so is the ability to think and remain flexible.

Captain Griffin had assigned the mission and when doing so, as he always did, told all of us why we were given the mission. Captain Griffin shared his "commander's intent" by adding "in order to keep the main supply route open for friendly forces" to the mission statement. Knowing the intent behind the task allowed us the freedom and confidence to make decisions at the ground level as the situation developed.

Confident we could make necessary changes to accomplish the mission, we acted decisively. The size of the existing perimeter was drastically reduced. We gave up the ice factory, hardened the ECPs, and dug our people and vehicles in. The terrain and our platoon's makeup made an exact "relief in place" impossible, but we knew our commander's intent. Knowing the reason we were given the assignment allowed us to adjust and construct a defensive position that complimented our capability. We endured constant IEDs, mortars, rockets, and small arms fire for the next two weeks, but our tactics worked. We held the position, secured the bridges, and disrupted insurgent activity in Karmah. Understanding the larger context of our actions empowered us to exercise initiative, remain flexible in a fluid environment, and ultimately accomplish the mission.

Marines are often thought of as robots, unable or not allowed to think for themselves and only capable of following orders. Crayon eaters, bullet sponges, window lickers, and knuckle draggers are common terms used to describe marines. I happily accept them all and even consider them terms of endearment from my fellow jarheads and combat veterans. My personal favorite is, "Instead of 'Semper Fi,' the marines should change their motto to 'Simpli Fi!'" I can accept and even laugh at this because I know the whole story. In battle, simplicity, aggressiveness, and execution determine victory. During my career, I have witnessed too many situations that were overthought and unnecessarily complex, when too many brains were trying to use the same scalpel when a sledgehammer was appropriate. Marines are not dumb; marine combat leaders are skilled tacticians, flexible, and cunning. They just do not mind swinging a sledgehammer when it's called for.

The stereotype that all marines are ASVAB waivers (the test required to enter all branches of the military) likely comes from a very stringent basic training where instilling discipline is one of the highest priorities. Movies like *Full Metal Jacket* and YouTube clips of drill instructors going ballistic on new recruits reinforce the stereotype that marines are only capable of doing exactly what they are told. The truth is exactly the opposite. Movies or clips on social media usually only depict the indoctrination process at the very beginning of the professional-development process of a US marine. After discipline, esprit de corps, and core values are instilled during basic training, all marines are expected to demonstrate initiative and become innovative and effective leaders through a formal professional-development process.

As any situation evolves, the ability to make decisions that deviate from initial instructions but are still in accordance with the overall goal is vital for anyone in a leadership role. The ability to do this in a challenging, fast-paced, and rapidly changing environment is what is required for success and survival during battle. Low-level leaders, noncommissioned officers, and first-line supervisors are and always will be the most important part of any organization. This class of leadership must be forward-thinking, innovative, and have the knowledge, ability, and *permission* to make decisions.

Innovative leaders able to adjust on the fly is not a new concept but often undervalued and underdeveloped, particularly in the private sector. An example of poor leadership within the ranks, with virtually no ability to think and act independently in accordance with the overall mission, was the Japanese Army on Guadalcanal during World War II. The fighting on Guadalcanal was intense jungle warfare, conducted in close quarters, often hand-to-hand. The dense terrain presented both challenges and solutions, depending on tactics. Marine Corps publication *FMFRP 12-110*, "Fighting on Guadalcanal," is an after-action report from front line marines and soldiers who led troops in combat during the Guadalcanal campaign. The publication was originally published in 1943. In their own words, marines and soldiers stressed the importance of knowing and using the commander's intent philosophy:

> If you shoot their officers (Japanese), they mill around. Their NCOs are poor.
>
> In their attacks and in their ground operations, the Japanese appear to follow very definite patterns. Each attack appears to be the same. They are easily disconcerted by surprise, and if they fail to succeed in what is apparently the only way they know how to fight, they become ineffective.

The Japanese soldiers were very disciplined and committed to the mission, but they lacked the ability or were not authorized to adjust the plans/tactics as the battle evolved. This inflexibility and inability to modify initial instructions at lower levels caused devastating losses. On one such occasion, Medal of Honor recipient Marine Sergeant John Basilone and his machine gun section were able to destroy almost an entire Japanese Regiment.

Marine Corps publication *FMFRP 12-110* also captures the value of instilling the idea of commander's intent in the marines and soldiers doing the fighting on Guadalcanal. Marines and soldiers had to make decisions on their own but in accordance with the overall mission. Commander's intent was probably not the term used in 1943, but the philosophy was alive and well and even encouraged.

The men have to be trained individually, for when the fighting starts, the corporal can't see all of his men.

The biggest thing I have learned since I hit this island is that leadership and initiative is so important here. The platoon leader can only be in one spot at a time, and the men must be trained to act correctly on their own.

We need trained soldiers that have initiative and know the right thing to do. The jungle here is so thick that the squad leaders cannot get around all of the time to see men and tell them what to do.

Sometimes the information doesn't get down to us and then we are really in the dark. When we get the orders and information we can get in there and pitch better.

These statements stress the value of teaching and implementing the commander's intent philosophy at the lowest levels. The Japanese missed out on the ingenuity, resourcefulness, and creativity their men possessed by overreliance and strict adherence to the initial plan developed by headquarters, not present and unable to adjust when the fighting commenced and the situation changed. US Forces recognized the talent and initiative within the ranks and as the after-action report shows, knew empowering all personnel with the knowledge and consent to make decisions independently based on real time information would drastically contribute to the success the mission. This concept was known in 1943 and has since been developed and refined. Commander's intent is one of the most important and powerful concepts successful leaders in any profession should implement and develop both personally and organizationally.

Younger generations are often maligned because they want to know the reason behind an assignment. The conversation during a staff meeting or training seminar usually goes something like this:

QUESTION: What is one of the biggest challenges you currently face in the workplace?

Response: It's this younger generation! They have to know why they are given every assignment. They should just do what they are told and not ask so many questions!

Almost instantly following the response, others in the room usually voice their agreement and add their two cents about how those younger than them are so needy and whiny because they want to know why they are being told to do a particular assignment. Often, the word *why* is instantly associated with younger generations and a negative connotation. I see it completely differently. I do acknowledge there are some serious situations when time does not permit any discussion and the instant-willing-obedience-to-all-orders approach is appropriate, but for the most part, there is plenty of time and good reason to explain why a task has been assigned.

Senior management who complains about youngsters asking *why* are in fact the ones doing the whining and possibly trying to redirect personal leadership failures onto their subordinates. If these same senior management personnel who have such a problem hearing *why* from their employees were presented with the concept of commander's intent or empowering employees through purpose, they would likely be receptive. Perhaps they would even implement those concepts personally or organizationally. "Commander's intent," "purpose," "context," and "why" are the same thing. The marines and soldiers who won the Battle of Guadalcanal were not millennials or Gen Zs. They were members of America's greatest generation, as tough as they come, and they asked why. In addition, the combat leaders who succeeded in leading their units to victory on Guadalcanal understood the significance of making sure the larger context of their mission or the *why* was known and understood, down to the man!

Commander's intent in some form is necessary to operate at a high level no matter the profession. Any time there are two opposing wills, the situation will be fluid, and whoever mentally and physically outpaces the other will gain the initiative and have a significant advantage. Superior tempo is established through efficiency, and one of the keys to efficiency is allowing subordinates the freedom to exercise judgment and initiative when the unexpected occurs. The ability to deviate from the original plan but stay focused on the overall objective establishes tempo. Operating faster than your opponent in this type of environment is crucial.

Imagine two containers of water on top of a mountain representing opposing wills. Both containers are simultaneously poured out on opposite sides of the mountain. Whichever container of water reaches the bottom of the mountain first is the victor. The mountain is very rocky, and as each stream of water moves down the mountain, they encounter friction. Each rock encountered, whether a pebble or a boulder, creates some level of friction. The water has to go right, left, over, or under every rock. Some rocks are sharp and may divide the water into two or more streams of water, continuing down the mountain and encountering friction on their own, separated from the main flow.

The friction on the mountain caused by the rocks is the same friction encountered in battle, a competitive market, or on a football field. In real life, each *rock* encountered represents an unforeseen challenge where the original direction is not possible or now obsolete and a decision has to be made to overcome the friction so progress can continue. The faster these decisions are made, the faster progress resumes. Thousands of small decisions across the workforce keep the water flowing toward the ultimate goal of reaching the bottom of the mountain first.

In any competitive environment, whichever team, unit, or organization can navigate the rocky environment faster while continuously making progress toward the desired end result outpaces their opponent and controls the outcome. The key to navigating down the mountain faster than the competition is empowering employees through commander's intent. There is no time for higher headquarters or executive leadership teams to make all the necessary decisions required to navigate the rocky terrain. These decisions must be made by those on the ground who are actually seeing the situation develop and equipped with real-time knowledge, and those decisions need to be based on the commander's intent.

Commander's intent is the mechanism that influences decisions made at the lower levels and achieves unity of effort across an organization. Effective leaders implement commander's intent by providing well-thought-out, clear, and concise instructions when issuing assignments using a mission statement. Every assignment, whether large or small, should have a structured mission statement attached to it. A structured mission statement has two parts: the task to be completed and the intent behind it. The task portion of a mission statement covers what needs to be done and may include when and where. The intent portion of a mission statement explains why the task is necessary. The intent is a necessary part to every mission statement, no matter how simple the task. Explaining why the task is necessary is the most important part of any mission statement. The purpose behind the task will remain long after the task is accomplished or becomes irrelevant.

The mission statement issued from Captain Griffin upon our reassignment was, "Move to this location, conduct a relief in place with the army Stryker platoon, and secure both strategic bridges in order to keep the main supply route open for friendly forces." The task portion of the mission statement is "move to this location, conduct a relief in place, and secure both strategic bridges." The intent portion is "in order to keep the main supply route open for friendly forces." Without the intent, we could have completely failed the mission while perfectly executing the task. Commander's intent not only guided the decision to reduce the Stryker platoon's perimeter but guided our actions for weeks.

A day into the assignment between Qaryat ash Shahabi and Al-Karmah, one of our patrols discovered an additional bridge two kilometers north of Karmah. Knowing our commander's intent was to "keep the main supply route open for friendly forces," this additional bridge became just as important to the mission as the two bridges we had originally been tasked with securing.

We didn't have enough manpower to divide our platoon and maintain a constant presence at all three bridges, so we began aggressively patrolling the area of the third bridge north of Karmah. We could have sat back and only accomplished the initial task, definitely the safer option, but in combat, the mission comes first.

Confident we were acting in accordance with the intent of our mission, we routinely and randomly left the relative safety of our defensive position to conduct day and night security patrols and establish listening and observation posts near the third bridge. We did our best to be offensive in nature and attempt to deter and disrupt insurgent activity to keep the supply route open, and we paid a price for it. We encountered several IEDs during our patrols. Some we found; some detonated, wounding marines and killing an army sergeant who was attached to us as an interpreter.

On one occasion, we found a daisy-chained IED (two devices connected to each other) on the third bridge north of Karmah. The IED had multiple 155-millimeter artillery rounds wired together and designed to explode simultaneously when detonated by an insurgent hiding in reeds along the canal bank. The device would have destroyed the bridge and whatever was on it. There is no doubt the device was meant for us. Our engineers were able to successfully disable and destroy the IED, keeping all the bridges intact and allowing the main supply route to stay open. Guided by commander's intent, we were able to exercise initiative, confidently deviate from the original plan, and ultimately accomplish the mission.

Successful leaders implement commander's intent both personally and organizationally. On a personal level, every leader in any profession, whether formal or informal, should seek to know and understand the intent of their supervisors. If a task is assigned and a supervisor does not provide a clear reason why the task is necessary, clarification should be sought. Execution should never begin until a clear understanding of the intent of supervisors from two levels above has been clearly communicated. Understanding commander's intent and using it to guide every decision achieves unity through an organization's structure.

Organizationally, leaders should value commander's intent not only for its ability to establish tempo, increase efficiency, and accomplish the mission but also for its ability to develop future leaders. Adopting the commander's intent philosophy is one of the most powerful tools for developing highly effective leaders who will lead an organization in the future. Commander's intent encourages decisiveness and ingenuity at the lowest levels and gives future supervisors and managers the opportunity to develop judgment and exercise initiative.

When empowering subordinates to become good and confident decision-makers through commander's intent, successful leaders should discuss and evaluate the decision-making process the subordinate used and refrain from solely evaluating outcomes. Only focusing on outcomes does not allow subordinates the chance to learn and grow. Instead, successful leaders should mentor their subordinates on the process they used that brought about the outcome and evaluate their intentions.

Makeshift sign leaving our platoon's position between the two bridges outside Karmah, Iraq. The smoke in the background is from an IED attack. This image was captured by an embedded reporter.

Chapter 9

Be Somebody or Do Something

Col. John Boyd was an air force fighter pilot who changed the modern battlefield forever. Boyd dedicated his life to developing tactics and strategy initially for air warfare, but his theory would grow in scope and become the model for ground combat tactics adopted by the marine corps. The American fighting style of maneuver warfare can be attributed to Boyd. "Fire and maneuver" and "fire and movement," two concepts every marine is taught, practiced, and executed against the enemy are a product of an eccentric air force fighter pilot.

Boyd concluded that whenever opposing wills engage, all competitors must navigate through the same decision-making cycle of observe, orientate, decide, and act. Known as the OODA loop, this decision-making cycle has come to guide actions not only on the battlefield but wherever a competitive environment exists. Whoever is able to operate more efficiently through the OODA loop wins. Maneuver warfare is just as much psychological as physiological. It is about outpacing the enemy mentally, causing catastrophic breakdowns and loss of control resulting in defeat, not from attrition but from incapacitation.

Though Boyd changed the modern battlefield forever, he was an oddity and not well liked by his superiors. He never promoted past the rank of colonel and died as an outcast of the air force and a hero to the marine corps. Boyd's challenges with his superiors were fueled by his rigid adherence to his personal values, and Boyd valued getting things that needed to be done, done. Boyd did not "play the game" well. He never even played the game. He was uncompromising.

Boyd operated against the grain, choosing hard work and results over position and accolades. He once counseled a junior officer under his command, saying,

> One day you will come to a fork in the road and you're going to have to make a decision about which direction you want to go…If you go that way you can be somebody. You will have to make compromises and you will have to turn your back on your friends. But you will be a member of the club and you will get promoted and you will get good assignments…or you can go that way and you can do something- something for your country and for your Air Force and for yourself.

Boyd had a deep understanding of the importance of guarding against false idols. He was witness to ambitious leaders falling for the same pitfalls time and again, leaders who took the easy road and "played the game," choosing position over purpose, recognition over results, and ego over humility.

Successful leaders have to be self-aware and continually evaluate intentions. It's easy for talented and ambitious people to be derailed or corrupted by early success, titles, and paychecks, each without substance. Boyd's definition of success was to do something rather than be somebody, and he changed the world forever. Successful leaders must have a clear definition of what success is, constantly check their ego, and master the art of being humble.

In the first few days of November in 2004, the Light Armored Reconnaissance platoon I was assigned to was notified we would depart the next day and begin combat operations south of Fallujah in preparation for the all-out siege that was only days away. We were told we would not return to our patrol base on Camp Baharia until after the battle and to plan for eight to ten days in the field. So we made our final preparations, checked equipment, cleaned weapons, topped off vehicles, and packed our gear.

Eight to ten days in the field wasn't a terribly long time. I made sure I had a clean set of clothes to wear and packed two additional sets of undershirts, socks, and underwear. Each set was tightly rolled and stuffed into a Ziploc bag and sealed. Every three or four days, I would change my socks, undershirt, and underwear and change the outer uniform as needed. The used undergarments were rolled up tightly and pressed into the empty Ziploc bag. This process kept everything dry and organized inside my rucksack.

Twenty days later, I was sitting on the turret of a LAV-25, pulling my shift of fire watch and contemplating my dilemma. We had been conducting sustained combat operations around Fallujah for almost a month. We had no access to shower or laundry services and had long run through what we packed. We must have been a sight to see. Hair was way out of regulation, one of my boot soles was held on by duct tape, paracord replaced both boot laces, the crotch was ripped out of my last set of fatigues, and I had been wearing the same socks, underwear, and undershirt for almost two weeks. We were clean-shaven, but we were filthy.

The dilemma was trying to decipher the results of the sniff test I had performed repeatedly for the past hour or so. The stench stemming from my body had become a significant distraction. I retrieved both Ziploc bags from my rucksack that contained my previously worn undergarments. I opened each bag and smelled their contents then myself to see what the better option was. There was no obvious choice. Since I had nothing but time on my hands, I continued to perform the sniff test until I eventually accepted the harsh reality. The used items marinating in a Ziploc bag for weeks were the better option, so I made the switch.

Combat is often romanticized on television and movie screens. In actuality, combat is the most unromantic environment imaginable. Most forms of media, whether fiction or nonfiction, tend to focus on the highlights and dramatic action scenes where the hero is victorious, the same scenes that American kids replicate when waging all-out war with other kids using rifles made from sticks and pine cones as hand grenades. A movie or television program that depicted combat with complete accuracy would be anything but entertaining. There is no glory in the physical and mental toll combat demands, only perspective.

Combat is one of the most effective teachers of humility. Combat can make anyone or anything seem small. The size and scope of two countries killing each other, the fragility of the human body, and observing firsthand how common, random, and futile death is creates a sobering view of one's personal importance, or lack thereof, within the universe. Combat has a way of putting things in perspective by forcing harsh reality into every situation. Inflated egos do not do well or last long in battle. Either humility is learned quickly, or the inflated ego dies with its host.

Successful leaders have to keep their ego in check. If not monitored, the ego can become inflated, creating an unhealthy and unrealistic view of one's self. No one is immune. Everybody has an ego. Some just do a better job managing it than others. Ego thrives in competitive environments, where aspiring people are motivated by wealth, recognition, and status. Unchecked ego is a vicious circle that plays out in an imaginary alternate universe. Ego is antireality. The number of families, businesses, organizations, and teams destroyed by ego is unfathomable.

Ego is sneaky. It creeps up on you because it feels good. It feels good to tell yourself you are the best or that you are right and everybody else is wrong. Take some ego and add in some success, and the problem becomes compounded. Success means recognition, accolades, power, money—all of which stroke the ego and fuel the fire of self-centered ambition. Ego must be tempered with capability. Did Michael Jordan have an ego when he was the best basketball player on the planet? Yes, but he was also the best basketball player on the planet. Training that enables first-level leaders to recognize and thwart the over inflated ego should be mandatory.

I will never forget one of the times (there have been many) my ego got the best of me. I was a young sergeant (E-5) temporarily assigned as a troop handler for new marines attending their military occupational specialty (MOS) School. I had had some success. I was promoted quickly, received a few awards, and was thriving on the *attaboys* and praise received from my superiors. I was going places. I had a big head fueled by an ego that was out of control. The day of reckoning came unexpectedly when I pushed a little too hard. The details are meaningless. I overstepped my boundaries trying to show off and maintain my reputation as an up-and-comer.

I was summoned to a master gunnery sergeant's (E-9) office a few buildings down from mine. On the way over, my ego was still shielding me from reality and I even remember preparing myself to stand my ground and give the "with all due respect, master guns" intro. I entered the building and knocked on the halfway opened master gunnery sergeant's office door. The master gunnery sergeant asked who it was. I replied, "Sergeant Shaw."

The master gunnery sergeant yelled at the top of his lungs, "Report!"

This was not usually necessary outside of boot camp or disciplinary proceedings. Regardless, I reported, marching into the office, centered myself on the desk, and stated, "Good afternoon, master gunnery sergeant. Sergeant Shaw reporting as ordered."

My ego was still intact, and I was still prepared to make my case until the master gunnery sergeant caught me off guard by asking, "You play poker, motherf———?"

I was not anticipating the question nor the tone. I didn't have time to answer, and the surprised look on my face turned into the thousand-yard stare of a first-phase recruit at Parris Island when the master gunnery sergeant answered for me, "Because E-9s beat E-5s all f——— day!"

I then received the finest old-school marine corps ass chewing ever, and I deserved every bit of it. The whole building heard it and probably some marines outside of the building. To this day, when checking my ego, I still ask myself if "I'm playing poker?" I was humbled.

Humility is what keeps the ego in check and is necessary for someone to reach their potential as a leader. Humility requires extreme inward honesty. It's the willingness to accurately evaluate one's personal ability and importance. Countless leadership failures can be attributed to highly talented and motivated people not being inwardly honest and choosing to view themselves through a distorted lens that conveniently provides an illusion of capability and self-importance.

Humility requires being firmly grounded in reality. Humility requires acknowledgment of failures, inadequacies, and mediocracy, and in the acknowledgment lies the opportunity for improvement. There's a reason the marine corps first leadership principle is "know yourself and seek self-improvement." The marine corps wants its leaders to view themselves and the situation from a humble perspective. It's how we get better. It allows us to lead ourselves and others more effectively. Humility is also the key to being able to accept guidance and criticism from others, further increasing leadership ability.

The art of being humble is often and easily overlooked. Humility is earned. It is easily recognizable in mature, experienced leaders who have built a foundation on actual accomplishments instead of a deceptive ego. I've seen it on the battlefield, and I've seen it in law enforcement. It's the calm and quiet leader who exhibits competence and confidence without making a show of it, sharply contrasting with someone who is easily excitable and overwhelmed, driven by emotions instead of relevant experience and logic. No matter the profession, there is never a shortage of ambition, talent, or work ethic, but there will always be a shortage of humility.

Seven years after the Second Battle of Fallujah, I was watching what was happening in the city American marines and soldiers had sacrificed so much for. Fallujah was crumbling. The Iraqi Army had failed miserably at protecting Fallujah from a variety of terrorist groups, including Al-Qaeda, ISIS, and Sunni insurgents. Eventually, Fallujah would fall and remain under terrorist control for over two years. In 2016, the Iraqi army would conduct a major offensive operation and regain control of the city but with devastating effects on progress and infrastructure.

Watching Fallujah fall was a hard process for all those who had invested so much into liberating it in 2004. For months, I was obsessed with reading every article or watching any footage or news broadcast I could find. I could not believe the Iraqi government was willing to walk away. What about the Gold Star Families of the marines and soldiers who died there? What about the Iraqi people who endured years of fighting and chaos? What about me and my efforts? Though my contribution was tiny compared to so many others, the Second Battle of Fallujah changed my life. I was angry and stayed angry for some time until one day I realized I needed some of my own medicine. To be someone or to do something? Ego was shielding me from reality, and at some point, my perception of the unfolding events had become warped.

Fallujah fell; so what? That didn't make me less of a marine. It certainly didn't mean that the sacrifices of so many were meaningless, and it doesn't change how Gold Star Families should value the sacrifice of their sons, daughters, wives, husbands, brothers, and sisters. The success was from the effort. The achievement was the work. The victory was the sacrifice. The marines and soldiers who fought in Fallujah did everything asked of them. They won every battle, firefight, fistfight, stare down—whatever. We all did our job, and we did it well. We did something.

Anyone with the desire to reach their potential and lead others well must have a clear definition of what success is. Defining success is about doing something, not being somebody. Being somebody is ego driven; doing something is purpose driven. Personal ambition of recognition, titles, and wealth is egotistical and easily lost or stripped away. Then what? Accomplishments from fulfilled purpose last forever, just as the honor from the sacrifice of the marines and soldiers who took Fallujah will last forever in the legacy that lives on in today's marines.

Success should only be measured internally based on effort. Not getting the position, pay raise, award, or desired outcome should not determine success or failure. If it does, you have an ego problem. Knowing that the effort you gave, the work you put in, and the integrity you displayed meet your own personal standards is success. Dwelling on anything else is pointless and a complete waste of time. Col. John Boyd understood this and chose to do something, not chase a spot on an organizational chart.

In 2018, the World Wrestling Championships were held in Budapest, Hungary. Jordan Burroughs, one of the most accomplished freestyle wrestlers of all time from the United States, was the heavy favorite in the seventy-kilogram weight class. Burroughs lost in the quarterfinals, shocking wrestling fans around the world. He battled back through the bracket, won a hard-fought match, and took bronze. Immediately following the match, still dripping sweat and out of breath, Burroughs said,

> I never thought I would be happy to win a bronze medal. Things don't always go the way you want them. My life is purposeful. Whether it's first place or third place, I'm a happy man. Sometimes when you can't get want you want, you got to get what you can.

Burroughs easily accepted what the wrestling community considered a failure. He knew the work he put in, he knew how hard he trained, and he met his personal standard of excellence and fulfilled his purpose. Burroughs did something.

In Marcus Aurelius's book *Meditations*, Aurelius wrote, "Ambition means tying your well-being to what other people say or do. Self-indulgence means tying it to the things that happen to you. Sanity means tying it to your own actions." Success is in the effort. Make your actions count. Keep your head down, work hard, do your job, and go through the doors that open up along the way. Defining success on purposeful actions and effort provides stability for when life happens and you don't get what you thought was coming to you. Relying on outside influencers for personal validation is destined for an epic failure. Succeed, grow, and improve during a perceived failure by giving it your all. Maintain your integrity, your dignity. Check the ego, and do something.

Chapter 10

Semper Gumby

In mid-December of 2004, the heavy fighting inside Fallujah had subsided. The enemy stronghold had been pacified by the major offensive operation referred to as the Second Battle of Fallujah. Some marine units were still working to clear out small pockets of die-hard insurgents who somehow managed to survive the relentless onslaught of the battle. Fighting was sporadic, and inside Fallujah may have been the safest place in Iraq at the time. The city was essentially locked down and completely under US control.

The Marine Light Armored Reconnaissance platoon I was assigned to had been conducting combat operations since the beginning of November. We had endured a suicide car bomb, many improvised explosive devices, firefights, and continual indirect fire from rockets and mortars. The staggering operational tempo combined with the constant violence and danger transformed us into a seasoned combat unit. We were a well-oiled machine accustomed to what would have previously caused concern. We knew where to focus our attention. We could anticipate each other's thoughts and actions. Nothing surprised us or caught us off guard. The marines of Third Platoon now had that same hardened look of the Delta Company marines we had replaced four months earlier. We had become professional combat soldiers.

Alpha Company consisted of three-line platoons augmented by a weapons platoon and headquarters platoon. Each line platoon consisted of four light armored vehicles (LAV-25s). Each LAV-25 had three crew members and four specially trained infantry scouts.

In December, Alpha Company received orders to occupy the peninsula immediately west of Fallujah. Known as the shark fin, the peninsula was a point of land created by a sharp bend in the Euphrates River, which paralleled Fallujah on its west side. The peninsula was close enough to Fallujah, it was virtually uninhabited because of the heavy fighting that had taken place. Residents fled the area, and most had not returned.

Each platoon was assigned a section of the peninsula and instructed to establish a makeshift patrol base from an uninhabited structure. Our main mission was to prevent indirect fire coming from the peninsula into Fallujah proper. The intent was to limit disruptions inside Fallujah so the city could be reinhabited and elections could take place without incident.

Third Platoon was assigned the sector of the peninsula closest to the city. We had an additional mission to maintain security on the Euphrates River, allowing nothing to pass. We established a patrol base in a large house inside a walled compound previously occupied by another marine unit. The house sat directly on the Euphrates River, allowing us to maintain a presence in our assigned sector and also observe any activity on the river while staying together as a platoon.

We immediately went to work hardening the building with whatever materials we could manage. We covered the windows with blankets and plywood, strung concertina wire around the perimeter walls, built defensive positions on the roof, and rigged trip flares in key locations and dead space (areas not able to be observed). We also had combat engineers deliver demolitions and blew fields of fire through mature date palm groves bordering our position.

Our previous experience in Karmah had taught us to not take preparation lightly when preparing a defensive position. Two LAVs were stationed on the bank of the river, one facing north and one facing south. Each was manned twenty-four hours a day with standing orders to destroy any thing navigating the river that was not our own.

Once in place, we conducted routine security patrols in our assigned sector to maintain a presence and disrupt insurgent activity. Our company commander, Capt. John Griffin, a skilled tactician and dedicated war fighter, requested a marine intelligence unit known as a Human Exploitation Team (HET). The HET hit the ground running and soon developed actionable intelligence on insurgent activity on the peninsula. We began conducting midnight raids on houses and compounds, rounding up the insurgents who were responsible for building and emplacing improvised explosive devices (IEDs) and launching mortars and rockets into Fallujah.

The HET's efforts were so effective that they were able to turn two tribes against each other. Each tribe began informing us about the other's insurgent activity. We had solid intelligence about where IEDs had been emplaced and who was coordinating the insurgent activity in our area of responsibility. Numerous significant detainees were taken into custody, and we discovered several IEDs and weapons caches.

Some of the IEDs were very large in comparison to what was commonly encountered. One IED had multiple 155-millimeter artillery rounds on each corner of a four-way intersection and would have been catastrophic if detonated on anything other than an M1A1 Abrams tank. It was clear our LAVs were being specifically targeted by insurgents, and we would have to adjust to avoid a catastrophic IED attack.

Because of the significant IED threat, we drastically changed our tactics. The limited number of roads on the peninsula made it easy for insurgents to pattern our movement. There were only a few options in and out of our patrol base, and we didn't have the manpower to maintain a constant presence outside the wire. Continuing with our current tactics would have been the equivalent of pounding a square peg into a round hole. It wouldn't have been wrong; after all, we were a light armored infantry unit. Our vehicles were our main weapon system, but marines would have been killed and equipment destroyed.

Thankfully, our leadership was flexible in thought. Instead of continuing with the same tactics and essentially accepting the risk out of ease or ignorance, Captain Griffin and the rest of our command element took the time and made the effort to think outside the norm and accomplish the mission while mitigating and in some cases, eliminating the threat.

Platoons were reorganized into traditional infantry squads and day and night security patrols were conducted on foot. On foot, we lacked the firepower and protection of the armored vehicles that had shielded us from IEDs, rockets, mortars, and automatic weapons fire for months, but we were not limited in our movement. Patterning our foot patrols was virtually impossible, and the likelihood of locals allowing insurgents to emplace IEDs in their farm fields or on or near critical infrastructure was low.

For the next six weeks, we effectively patrolled our assigned portion of the peninsula without any significant incidents. We met with local tribal leadership and established rapport. We were even invited into some of their homes to eat with them. We learned that most of the permanent residents in the area were friendly or at least indifferent to the US presence and just wanted to get back to normal. Many were eager to vote and elect their government for the first time in their lives. Local leadership explained that many of the insurgents were from out of town or from other countries and came to Iraq only for the opportunity to kill Americans. Insurgents were intimidating the locals and occupying their towns and villages, threatening to kill anyone who provided information about their whereabouts to US forces.

Understanding the predicament the local populace was in, Captain Griffin decided to conduct a bold operation in a populated section just south of the shark fin, a decent-sized village surrounded by rich farmland irrigated from the Euphrates. Intelligence gathered from our attached HET indicated some of the last remaining insurgents on the peninsula were living in the village, and villagers would not provide any information out of fear of retaliation by the insurgents. The operation was to assist the village by ridding them of the insurgents and their ruthless intimidation tactics.

We received our operations order, and each platoon was assigned a section of the village in which to clear and search every structure.

Every military-aged male was to be taken into custody and brought back to our company command post for questioning. This way, no villagers were in danger for revealing the insurgents, and our HET knew the appropriate questions to ask to determine who belonged in the area and who did not.

Early the next morning, each element of Alpha Company patrolled to their assigned section and began systematically clearing every structure in broad daylight. All males from sixteen to sixty-five were detained and brought to a predetermined collection point. My squad alone must have cleared fifteen to twenty structures.

The unconventional approach and boldness of the operation caught the insurgents completely by surprise. Not a single shot was fired all day. As the sun was setting, we had dozens of military-aged males in our company headquarters area, waiting to be questioned by our intelligence marines. After it was all said and done, the insurgents who had come from near and far to kill Americans and torment the local populace were in custody and transported to Abu Ghraib Prison. The others returned to their homes that night.

After the large-scale operation in the southern peninsula, we shifted our focus to building upon the trust and confidence that had recently been established and began conducting more missions focused on humanitarian efforts in the area. This period is one of the greatest examples of flexibility I have ever witnessed. I was beyond fortunate to be a part of this special group of warriors, most still in their late teens and early twenties at the time. Repeatedly, these young and combat-hardened marines, poised to instantly engage the enemy with overwhelming violence and prejudice, would tactically and methodically bump and bound through broken urban terrain, where danger lurked around every corner, until reaching their objective, establish a perimeter, and smile as they slung their weapons to pass out soccer balls and candy to children and food and water to local families in need.

As the soccer game played out, the village elders would be greeted, and discussions took place as to any critical needs the village may have. The smaller Iraqi children would cling to us and ask to have their picture taken. During these moments, the dusty streets of

Iraq almost resembled a neighborhood block party in the States. The ability of young marines, who were barely considered adults, to transition from a combat patrol with deadly intentions to an innocent soccer game in the middle of a war zone is one of the unique qualities of the American marine and soldier.

Flexibility

The flexibility shown by the marines and company leadership on the peninsula is what directly contributed to an overwhelmingly successful mission. Combat is fluid. Scenarios may be similar, but they will never be identical. Each episode presents its own unique challenges shaped by the terrain, the enemy's will, and internal capability. The nature of combat demands flexibility of thought. War is a constant grind, like wading through a dense swamp with no idea of where the high ground is, only a direction of travel, and with every step, there is an unforeseen obstacle. Thick trees, sunken logs, predators all have to be negotiated while the soft mud and relentless heat bogs you down, draining energy and resources.

Friction is the official term the marine corps uses to reference the extreme adversity encountered during war. Friction cannot be taught to the level it will be experienced. It can only be replicated in battle. Friction mandates constant problem-solving. Mental flexibility is the only way to overcome friction. The inability to quickly and effectively adapt in combat will rapidly lead to frustration and bewilderment. Combat leaders must be proactive and flexible to shape the battlefield to their advantage and constantly react as the situation changes.

Successful leaders in any capacity have the poise to see through the chaos, decipher what action is necessary, and the mental flexibility to quickly take corrective action. Situations involving friction rarely present a perfect solution. Leaders capable of flexibility of thought recognize opportunities for compromise and quickly seize on promising courses of action to skillfully execute.

Purpose

German philosopher Friedrich Nietzsche said, "He who has a why to live for can bear almost any how." Your *why* is your purpose. It is what fuels the commitment that turns a promise into a reality. The marine corps understands this. Every marine is instilled with a strong sense of purpose through the grueling process of earning the Eagle, Globe, and Anchor. Duty, honor, and sacrifice combine to create a strong desire for every marine to uphold the legacy and traditions of those who wore the uniform before them. This shared sense of purpose contributes to the unbreakable bond shared among marines, brothers and sisters in arms committed to the mission and committed to each other.

Instilling a sense of purpose into every marine is an integral part of basic training but not exclusive to the marine corps. No matter the profession or position, purpose is necessary for long-term success and well-being. Dreams and aspirations can quickly be shattered because passion and motivation are mistaken for purpose and discipline. Operating with passion looks good, but operating with purpose functions good!

To understand your purpose, you have to understand what is important to you, what you value, and what your aspirations are. Purpose is easily identified in combat. It's required for survival. For people without structured military training, purpose can sometimes be illusive. Most professions are not noble or glamorous on the surface, so it's easy to be shortsighted and focus too much on challenges associated with an actual task instead of the purpose behind performing the task.

Identifying purpose requires taking the time to recognize the reason for performing a task, the need behind the need. Using the workplace as an example, the need is to have a steady job that provides financial stability. Recognizing the need behind the need reveals the purpose. Stopping at the need to have a steady job does nothing to contribute to the resilient mindset. The need behind the need varies from person to person but is what brings meaning to the work. Focusing only on the need to have a steady job leads to frustration and burnout when the work itself is the sole focus and becomes mundane and monotonous. The need behind the need for a steady job is what should be focused on when the going gets tough. That's where the inner strength to continue performing carries you through adversity. The need behind the need is your purpose. You need a steady job because the rent is due, because you need tuition for college so you can replace your supervisor, because you want a better life for your children, etc. Find your purpose and focus on it rather than the task.

Emotional intelligence

In the spring of 2005, our unit, Alpha Company, was quickly closing in on the end of our deployment. One of the requirements before departure was a briefing from the regimental chaplain. All members of Alpha Company made their way to Camp Fallujah and reluctantly filed into the makeshift auditorium. The regimental chaplain introduced himself and began explaining what returning to the States would entail. He used himself as an example and explained how he had been granted leave to go home for a couple of weeks during his deployment. He told us during his time at home, he would hear machine guns in the distance and explosions that turned out to be normal sounds of everyday life upon further investigation. He described his interaction with his family and children and how his combat experiences caused strain on personal relationships.

As young marines wrapping up a tough deployment, we thought we were bulletproof mentally and physically. We laughed and made jokes about the chaplain and his message. Discussions about mental health were taboo in 2005, and no one had heard of the term post-traumatic stress.

I returned home from Iraq in the spring of 2005. We flew into Cherry Point, North Carolina, and were bussed to our battalion area at Camp Lejeune. It was late at night when we arrived. Friends and family members were there to celebrate our return. My wife, Crystal, welcomed me off the bus, and hugging her that night will always be one of my fondest memories. I asked that no one else attend the welcome home ceremony. I just wanted to spend time with Crystal and for some reason felt nervous about seeing anyone else. My parents were not pleased, but I insisted. This was my first inclination that something was not quite right. During the months that followed, more issues would present themselves.

I couldn't sleep, was paranoid, and would break out in a heavy sweat when in public. I felt detached, numb, confused, and all of a sudden, I developed a temper. I had always been very easygoing, like water off a duck's back, but relatively minor things would now send me into a rage.

On one occasion, while assisting with a corporal's leadership course hosted at our battalion headquarters, a junior marine from another unit disrespected, in my opinion, our company first sergeant, First Sergeant Link. First Sergeant Link epitomized the marine company first sergeant. He was a mentor to me and dedicated to his marines.

I noticed the incident and went over to First Sergeant Link as fast as I could. As I got closer, the junior marine continued to act defiantly, and when I got close enough, I erupted! I began screaming at the marine, making my way closer, eventually ending the tirade by labeling him a moo-moo shit-bird m———f———er and attempting to strike him right there on the battalion parade deck, in broad daylight, in front of everyone. Luckily, First Sergeant Link got hold of me before I was able to grab the kid and told him to get the hell out of here. I was in such a state of rage, I think I would have killed the guy if I had gotten to him.

I did my best to mask the way I was feeling, but it must have been obvious to those around me. Crystal even set up a private meeting with First Sergeant Link to discuss my behavior. She never told me about the meeting until years later because she knew notifying my chain of command of the issues I was having would have infuriated me. First Sergeant Link told her to give it time and that everyone was having similar experiences.

In the summer of 2005, I received orders for recruiting duty and attended recruiters school in San Diego. I was eager for a new start and a new assignment to keep my mind occupied. Recruiting school and recruiting duty are not for everybody. The school focuses heavily on public speaking and selling skills. My barracks roommate quickly failed out and was sent back to the Fleet Marine Force, allowing me to have my own room.

What would have been a blessing for most was a nightmare for me. The next six weeks, unless in class, would be spent alone in a barracks room, unable to sleep, scared and determined to let no one find out how bad I was feeling. Failing or dropping out of recruiters school would have resulted in a negative fitness report, eliminating any future chance of promotion. That's when I turned to alcohol as self-medication. I had always been a social drinker, but this was different. I began drinking with a purpose, and the purpose was to calm down and sleep.

As it turned out, a negative fitness report wouldn't have mattered. In November of 2007, my enlistment contract was up, and I decided to get out of the marines after eight and a half years. Recruiting duty was challenging enough by itself, but coupled with the negative effects and emotions I was feeling from combat made service almost unbearable. Crystal and I had a newborn baby girl and were constantly fighting. All I saw in my mind was combat, every day, all day. Working, speaking, watching television—it didn't matter. I would carry on full conversations while simultaneously reliving a firefight, IED blast, or mortar attack in my mind. I never told anybody. I just left everyone wondering why I was so quiet and angry all the time and became more and more detached.

The only job I could find in the small town we settled in after getting out of the marine corps was working on seawalls for a marine construction company. The job didn't pay well, but it was forty hours a week, and we needed the money. I didn't care for the job or my coworkers, many of whom were parolees, hard drug users, and sketchy lowlifes. But the job turned out to be an unknown blessing, and the blessing was the hard work. At work, my mind would start its Iraq reruns, and I would relive my combat experiences but take the anger it caused and focus it on whatever needed built or destroyed. I was every boss' dream. I never called off, kept to myself, and would outwork anyone.

Working, exercising, and drinking—the stubborn fool's guide to dealing with post-traumatic stress. I would swing a 20 lb. hammer all day busting concrete seawall cap then come home and run five miles or bike to a public pool to swim laps. When finished, I would start drinking. Working and exercising helped me handle the *reruns* that I could not figure out how to turn off, and drinking helped me sleep and feel somewhat human again.

At the time, I only had two emotions: I felt nothing or I was angry. If I drank enough, I could feel happy and enjoy playing with the kids and spending time with Crystal. I was trying to be a good father and husband. I just had no emotions while doing it. Ashamed of myself for the way I was feeling, I knew something was really wrong, but my pride would not allow me to ask for help. Seeking help for mental health and wellness was a sign of weakness to me and completely out of the question, so I did what far too many people do. I kept working, exercising, and drinking for the next decade.

Desperation overcame my pride when Crystal told me she had had enough. Crystal was and still is everything to me. We were high school sweethearts and married at nineteen. She is an incredibly loving and supporting wife and mother, but she was at her limit and rightfully so. That is when I did the most difficult thing I have ever done and met with a therapist I found online who had previous experience working with veterans.

The first time I met with Dr. Riccardi was a terrible experience for me and probably for her too. I was so ashamed of myself and embarrassed for being there, I don't remember saying much. Looking back, I am surprised Dr. Riccardi made another appointment. We met once a week for a couple of months, and I slowly began to loosen up but eventually stopped going because of the cost. I could have gone to the Veterans Administration for free, but I didn't want a diagnosis in my jacket, didn't want to be a disabled veteran, didn't want compensation, and didn't want medication. I wanted help.

Unbeknownst to me, Crystal reached out to Dr. Riccardi about options to get me back into her office. She told me Dr. Riccardi enrolled in a program through the VA that allowed her to treat a veteran at no cost, and she would be compensated through the VA. Crystal said Dr.

Riccardi had chosen me for the program so I could continue seeing her. I now know Crystal was full of it, and Dr. Riccardi agreed to see me at no cost out of kindness. Crystal knew I would not have accepted the services for free. Dr. Riccardi and I met regularly for the next three years, and she helped me deal with my combat experience. She taught me to recognize and acknowledge thoughts and emotions associated with the past and put them in perspective before they manifested into extreme anger, reruns, and depression.

I will be forever grateful for Dr. Riccardi. The concepts she taught helped me properly deal with my combat experiences, resulted in a heightened awareness of personal emotions, and began my first experience with emotional intelligence. Emotional intelligence (EI) is the ability of a person to recognize and manage their emotions. For some people, it probably comes naturally. For me, it did not. The ability to recognize and manage emotions took time, effort, and dedication. Emotional intelligence is not only beneficial for someone who experiences a traumatic event but is also necessary for overall well-being and high performance. Effectively recognizing and managing emotions leads to not being overwhelmed and overreacting when strong emotions are felt.

Emotional intelligence is essential to succeeding in a leadership position. The saying, "IQ gets you the job, and EI gets you promoted," is completely accurate. Successful leaders must make good decisions, treat people with respect, remain calm, and stay in control during high-stress situations. To do this, an increased level of self-awareness is necessary to understand how emotions affect personal behavior and behavior toward personnel. Leaders who are overwhelmed by fear, anger, embarrassment, jealousy, etc. will make hasty decisions and lash out based on strong emotions instead of making calculated decisions rooted in sound logic and principle.

Developing EI is more than recognizing an emotion. It's about deeply understanding why you are having the emotion. Analytic evaluation of emotions leads to a much deeper understanding of the situation, and no matter the situation, you always have the ability to choose your response. Developing EI is not easy. It is a process. It takes commitment, discipline, and humility to recognize the onset of certain emotions and then mentally and strategically pause to honestly examine why the emotion is present. Emotional intelligence requires self-awareness and self-restraint. Many times, honestly examining emotions leads to a realization that the anger, blame, or disappointment that you were about to direct outwardly at someone is actually a symptom used to mask personal fears or failures. EI requires complete inward honesty, discipline, and a ton of practice, but is well worth the effort and necessary to succeed at high levels.

Mental resiliency

> Do not believe that he who seeks to comfort you lives untroubled among the simple and quiet words that sometimes do you good. His life has much difficulty and sadness... Were it otherwise he would never have been able to find those words. (Rainer Maria Rilke)

Of all the chapters in this book, this is the one I wish I could have read prior to my combat experience, like a letter sent back to my younger self. There's no way I could have accurately comprehended war prior to experiencing it. I can say there were times I felt desperately overwhelmed and inadequate but thankfully never in the moment because my training and the marines to my right and left proved sufficient. The mental burden became apparent during the lulls of combat and more prevalent after the fighting had stopped. Focusing on and developing a resilient mindset prior to combat would have served me well. The intangible aspect of war is just as significant on the battlefield as the physical aspect, but the intangible aspect is permanent.

Years of reflection on combat experiences coupled with personal and professional development and a strong desire to understand the intangible aspect, consequence, and benefit of combat have led me to believe that mindset—whether on the battlefield, the boardroom, or locker room—is just as important as any physical skill set. Mindset is what matters after adversity, and adversity is inevitable. Our mindset is the foundation that all our physical skills are built upon and the chassis that brings those skills to bear. Without proper mindset, there is no preparation, execution, or follow-through—all as equally as important as the other.

In the marine corps, there is a common phrase known as "Semper Gumby." All marines are familiar with it and hear it for the first time early on during basic training. It is a staple in marine corps jargon. *Semper* is Latin for "always." Gumby refers to a fictional humanoid character fashioned out of green clay, made famous during a 1980s television show. Gumby, being made from clay, was naturally flexible and would bend and contort as the situation demanded. So the term "Semper Gumby," for marines, translates to "always flexible."

On the surface, "Semper Gumby" simply means to always remain flexible and at lower levels on an organizational chart usually suffices as a way to communicate to subordinates that plans will or have changed. While the character Gumby was physically flexible, Semper Gumby refers to mental flexibility and implies the need to accept change and try and make the best of it—simple on the surface but extremely complex in reality! Successful leaders in any profession must come to understand the full scope of the situation and the effects it will have on their people.

Instructing someone to remain flexible is nowhere near adequate. Semper Gumby involves much more than remaining flexible. Marines understand the concept as a holistic, resilient mindset necessary to properly prepare for, perform during, and recover from situations of extreme adversity. In combat, it's a way of life, usually forced, and a hard lesson learned in the most trying environments. Outside of combat, mindset is a choice and an area of focus successful leaders have to be proactive in developing internally and instilling into others.

Semper Gumby is the mindset marines use to cope with challenging and sometimes horrific circumstances. It is the resilient mindset. It has proven successful on battlefields all over the world. Though extremely common, the expression is not the most endeared phrase to marines because it always precedes or follows bad news, a change of plans, or an unexpected occurrence that presents a new challenge or obstacle. Synonymous with "overcome and adapt," another commonly used expression in the marines and other branches of the military, both attempt to communicate the need to expect and accept the unexpected, thrive in uncertainty and after adversity, then endure the permanent and invisible scars of war.

A resilient mindset is a leadership concept and skill that can and should be developed and maintained by anyone aspiring to lead others well. But more than that, a resilient mindset is about quality of life. The benefits apply equally to everyone. The single mother working two jobs to keep the lights on and the family fed benefits the same as the combat leader by adopting the Semper Gumby concept. Whether conquering life or the enemy, everything is at stake, and the show must go on. The key to developing a resilient mindset is having a purpose then understanding and implementing flexibility and emotional intelligence.

Flexibility + Purpose + Emotional Intelligence = Resilient Mindset.

Flexibility, purpose, and emotional intelligence are the combination that contributes to developing a resilient mindset, and a resilient mindset is what separates those who do the job briefly from those who excel at the job perpetually. Mindset is what matters after adversity, and adversity is guaranteed. The ancient Roman emperor and philosopher Marcus Aurelius wrote, "You have the power over your mind-not outside events. Realize this, and you will find strength." Effective leaders and anyone else who desire to reach their potential, succeed at higher levels, maintain quality of life, and gracefully endure life's struggles will come to understand and pursue the resilient mindset.

Author pictured with local children during a foot patrol
on the southern portion of the peninsula.

About the Author

Barry Shaw enlisted in the marine corps immediately following high school in July 1998. He served two enlistments until November 2007. During the second enlistment, Shaw was a vehicle commander for a light armored vehicle assigned to Alpha Company, Second Light Armored Reconnaissance Battalion in Camp Lejeune, North Carolina. He deployed to Iraq in August 2004 attached to Regimental Combat Team 1 and fought in sustained combat operations in and around Fallujah until April 2005, participating in Operation Phantom Fury (the Second Battle of Fallujah). He was awarded the Navy and Marine Corps Commendation Medal with Combat "V" for his actions during the operation.

After leaving the marine corps in November 2007, Shaw, with his wife, moved to Florida and accepted a position as a conservation law enforcement officer with the Florida Fish and Wildlife Conservation Commission. He has served as a field officer, training lieutenant, advanced and in-service training captain, captain over statewide operations and professional standards, and currently serves as the Training Center Director.

Over the course of his fifteen-year career in law enforcement, Shaw has continued the professional-development process and in doing so, evaluated his combat experience, particularly his time in Fallujah. Reflection, practical application, and years of personal growth have enabled him to share his combat experiences and the practical leadership lessons those experiences provided.

Shaw has been married for twenty-five years and has two children active in competitive sports. He currently lives in Tallahassee, Florida, and loves to spend time outdoors with his family. He completed his bachelor's degree in criminal justice in 2019.